The African-Americanization of the Black Diaspora in Globalization or the Contemporary Capitalist World-System

Paul C. Mocombe
Carol Tomlin
Christine Callender

University Press of America,® Inc.
Lanham • Boulder • New York • Toronto • Plymouth, UK

Copyright © 2017 by University Press of America,® Inc.
4501 Forbes Boulevard, Suite 200, Lanham, Maryland 20706
UPA Acquisitions Department (301) 459-3366

Unit A, Whitacre Mews, 26-34 Stannary Street,
London SE11 4AB, United Kingdom

All rights reserved
Printed in the United States of America
British Library Cataloguing in Publication Information Available

Library of Congress Control Number: 2016931323
ISBN: 978-0-7618-6721-0 (pbk : alk. paper)—ISBN: 978-0-7618-6722-7 (electronic)

∞™ The paper used in this publication meets the minimum requirements of American National Standard for Information Sciences Permanence of Paper for Printed Library Materials, ANSI/NISO Z39.48-1992.

Contents

Acknowledgments v

Introduction 1

1 Black Consciousnesses and Identities in America and the Diaspora 21
2 Phenomenological Structuralism 31
3 The Constitution of Modernity and Modern American Society via the Protestant Ethic and the Spirit of Capitalism 57
4 The Constitution of Black America within the Protestant Ethic and the Spirit of Capitalism 77
5 Conclusions: The Constitution of African and Caribbean Life within the Protestant Ethic and the Spirit of Capitalism 99

References Cited 121

Index 135

Acknowledgments

My analysis and conclusions are the result of the mentoring of two great professors, the late Drs. Stanford M. Lyman and Teresa Brennan; to them I owe my intellectual growth and framework. I would also like to thank Mt. Carmel/Erzulie, who I was name after, my spiritual Lwa or Saint in Haitian metaphysics, and my grandparents, Saul and Eugenia Mocombe, who taught me why and how to love.
Paul Camy Mocombe, May 3, 2012

I must thank my family, Beryl, Tony and mother, Sylvie and my church family Restoration Fellowship Ministries, for their enduring love. Special thanks go to Rev. Tamika Pusey Squire for her encouragement throughout this project. Last but by no means least my appreciation extends to the Lord Jesus Christ for being a continual source of inspiration.
Carol Tomlin May 11, 2012

For my mother Ermie, my late father Rupert and daughter, Natasha.
Christine Callender October 30 2015

Introduction

During slavery, colonialism, and decolonization within the emerging Protestant capitalist world-system of the sixteenth, seventeenth, eighteenth, nineteenth, and early twentieth centuries people of African descent in Africa and the diaspora were structurally differentiated along racial-class lines and forced to relationally constitute their being-in-the-world around their skin-color (blackness), lack of culture/civilization, and poor material conditions. Be that as it may, no matter what area of the world they were colonized or enslaved people of African descent were black and poor, and their leaders and intellectuals from Boukman Dutty, Jean-Jacques Dessalines, Alexander Pétion, Martin Robinson Delaney, Frederick Douglas, Henry Highland Garnett, Marcus Garvey, W.E.B. Du Bois, Ida B. Wells, Booker T. Washington, Carter G. Woodson, Patrice Lumumba, Thomas Sankara, etc., attempted to develop an universal conception of blackness around which all black people, in the absence of any black nation-state (outside of Haiti, which, because of its Revolution, was of great pride for black folks), should recursively reorganize and reproduce their being-in-the-world. Obviously, disagreements arose from the segregationist ideology of Booker T. Washington to Garveyite pan-Africanism, Haitian Black Nationalism, noirisme, créolité, and the assimilationist ideology of the "black bourgeoisie" (E. Franklin Frazier's term).

Abolitionism, desegregation, and decolonization resolved these competing political and sociological ideologies within the post-World War II capitalist world-system under American hegemony via the retrenchment of the nation-state system and the creation of black/African countries (nation-states) in Africa and the diaspora under the leadership of the black "comprador" bourgeoisie of slavery and colonialism (Frantz Fanon's term). As such, the dominant images and purposive-rationality of blackness became defined relationally by whites and the black bourgeoisies, i.e., a professional class of preachers, bureaucrats, administrators, entrepreneurs, managers, teachers, doctors, etc., interpellated and embourgeoised by the ideological apparatuses (churches, schools, streets, prisons, police forces) of the West, along the bourgeois line of whites seeking equality of opportunity, recognition, and distribution with their white counterparts. This urban black bourgeoisie, which would assume the leadership of their countries from their former colonial slavemasters, became differentiated along racial-class lines (a racial caste in class) from the rural and urban (slum) population of their respective countries and island nation-states. Based on the recommendations of the so-called post-WWII international community under American hegemony, they (the administrative black bourgeoisie) had to interpellate and embourgeois their masses as wage-laborers in capital determining organizations of work, i.e., agribusinesses, manufacturing, tourism, athletics, etc., in order to achieve their goal of equality of opportunity, recognition, and distribution with their white counterparts (Klak, 1998; Conway, 1998). Be that as it may, blackness became structurally differentiated in Africa, the diaspora, and former colonizing countries (the Metropoles) between a black bourgeoisie and an underclass both seeking equality of opportunity, recognition, and distribution as subjects/agents of the Protestant Ethic and the spirit of capitalism. Hence, whereas in most areas of the black diaspora (the Caribbean, Brazil, and Belize) the black bourgeoisie was differentiated from a black working and underclasses based fundamentally on class positions, In Haiti and Africa they encountered a rural population with different forms of system and social integration, which they discriminated against.

This work sets forth the argument that in this post-colonial age of globalization or the contemporary capitalist world-system under American (neoliberal) hegemony, the black bourgeoisies, working, and underclasses around the world, i.e., the black/African diaspora, are ever-so slowly becoming African-Americanized, i.e., interpellated, integrated, and embourgeoised within the amalgamated racial-class dialectic of black America. This African-Americanization—defined as the convergence of black folks around the world towards the amalgamated racial-class dialectic of black America—of Africa and the black diaspora is a result of three factors:1) Globalization; 2) black diasporic immigration to, or (convict) deportation from, the US and as such their incorporation into the class dialectic of black American society; and 3) the material influence, structural reproduction and differentiation, of the Protestant ethic and the spirit of capitalism promulgated throughout the diaspora by the two dominant social class language games of the black American community, the black underclass (Hip-Hop culture), led by criminals, street personalities, rappers, athletes, and other entertainers; and the black bourgeois educated professional, managerial, and entrepreneurial classes led by black American charismatic neoliberal bourgeois Protestant preachers and educated professionals like Juanita Bynum, Michael Eric Dyson, TD Jakes, Creflo Dollar, etc., speaking for and representing the black bourgeois (educated) professional classes.

In the globalizing process under American hegemony, the black administrative bourgeoisies, working classes, and underclasses of Africa and the black diaspora come to fall within these two dominant classes, black bourgeoisie and underclass, as they are constituted in black America. On the one hand, the former two are influenced by the language and ideology of black American charismatic liberal/conservative bourgeois Protestant preachers and professionals in the likes of Eddie Long, Michael Dyson, TD Jakes, Creflo Dollar, and Juanita Bynum whose prosperity gospel (economic gain for its own sake and material wealth as a sign of God's grace, salvation, and blessings) permeates throughout the black Protestant church leaderships of America, Africa, and the diaspora. On the other hand, the black poor youth (underclasses) of the cities of Africa and the diaspora influence and are influenced by black American underclass language and ideology represented in the language and ideology of criminals, street personalities, black rappers, entertainers, and athletes whose images, along with their bourgeois counterparts, are overrepresented in the media industrial complex of America.

Like in Africa and the Caribbean, these two dominant classes (representatives or the power elites of the black underclass and bourgeoisie) of black America are the product of racial-class divisions and capitalist social relations of production of the Protestant Ethic and the spirit of capitalism and its ideological apparatuses. Although on the surface the ideology, practical consciousness, and language of the two social class language games appear to oppose one another, given their interpellation via different ideological apparatuses (the church and schools for the former; and prisons, the streets, and athletic and entertainment industries for the latter). We argue, given the two groups' material wealth within the Protestant Ethic and the spirit of capitalism of corporate America and its ideological apparatuses, they do not. Both groups seek to recursively reorganize and reproduce the same underlying ideology and practical consciousness, the Protestant Ethic and the spirit of capitalism, and have become the bearers of ideological and linguistic domination in black America, the diaspora, and the world. As such, in the age of globalization, they are antagonistically, seeking to homogenize, via their amalgamated (black American and diasporic consciousness) language and ideological practices, black social behavior in the African diaspora around their social class positions, which represent two sides of the same coin. That is, contemporarily, we are suggesting, that the socialization of other black people in the diaspora within the capitalist world-system under American (neoliberal) hegemony ought to be examined against and within the dialectical backdrop and processes of this racial-class power dynamic and the cultural and religious heritage of the black American people responsible for this phenomenon of homogenization or convergence we are referring to as the "African-Americanization" of the black diaspora.

BACKGROUND OF THE PROBLEM

In the age of globalization, contemporarily, race and class distinctions in black communities throughout the diaspora are being constituted, i.e., interpellated, embourgeoised, and differentiated, by the language, ideology, and practical consciousness of two social class language games of black America, which are the product of the mode of production, communicative discourse, practical consciousness, language, ideology, and ideological apparatuses of the upper-class of owners and high-level executives of the US. The upper class of owners and high-level executives, based in the corporate community of developed countries like the United States, represent today's dominant bourgeois capitalist (corporate) class whose various distributive powers lead to a situation where their policies (discursive practices, i.e., neoliberal policies; mode of production; and ideological apparatuses, i.e., police force, education, urban streets, prisons, etc.) determine the "life chances" of not only local social actors, within the globalizing developed nation, but global ones as well. As William Domhoff (2002) points out in *Who Rules America*, "The routinized ways of acting in the United States follow from the rules and regulations needed by the corporate community to continue to grow and make profits" (Domhoff, 2002, pg., 181).

Globally, this action plays out through US dominated institutions such as the World Bank (WB), World Trade Organization (WTO), International Monetary Fund (IMF) etc., who prescribe fiscal, political, and social policies to countries in search of aid for development. These policies aid the corporate-driven agenda of the developed world (fits them within the structure of their social relations, i.e., the discourse of the Protestant ethic and its discursive practice, the Spirit of Capitalism), rather than the agenda of the developing countries: the establishment of "free" open markets as the basis for development and social relations in developing countries, whose markets when established are unable to compete with that of competitors in the West. They therefore get usurped by corporate capitalists of the West who take advantage of the labor force—which is cheapened in order to compete globally with other—cheaper—prospective markets—and other resources of the developing country, who must allow these investors into their country in order to pay back the debts they owe to the aforementioned international institutions lest they are declared ineligible for aid and development loans if they do not open up (liberalize) and secure their markets.

On one side of the political spectrum, this contemporary "disembeddedness" of the economy from society has been labeled globalization (market-driven as opposed to the post World War II development model, which emphasized economic replication, i.e., prescribed stages of economic development for developing countries, along the lines of the developed world—US and Europe) under the auspices of neoliberalism (McMichael, 2008; Portes, 1997; Klak, 1998). This common sense view tends to see globalization as both an ideological force (a conceptualization of the world [, i.e., establishment of markets as the basis for social relations]) and a material force (i.e., real transnational movements of capital and commodities). That is to say, from this "natural attitude" or perspective, globalization serves not only as a tool for investors to extract concessions from states, and for investors and states to extract concessions from workers and other citizens (Klak, 1998, pg. 5), but also as a means of socialization to the capitalist social relations of production as the constitutive "practical consciousness" of modern societies. This is an ideological position, which assumes a distinction between the "life-world" of cultural meanings and subjective experiences, and the capitalist non-cultural, but rational, system, which "organically" governs them as a result of politically arrived at neo-liberal agreements that require countries to privatize and deregulate their economies, open up their markets to foreign direct investment, remove trade barriers and other neoliberal (structural adjustment) policy prescriptions mandated by the IMF, World Bank, the United Nations, etc., under the auspices of American hegemony (Habermas, 1984 [1981]; Klak, 1998; McMichael, 2008).

On the other side of the political spectrum, this same position amounts to a (neo) liberal euphemism for Immanuel Wallerstein's (1974) Marxist world-systems theory, which emphasizes the integration of the world into a functional system "based on capitalist commodity production organized by a world market in which both purely economic competitive advantage and political interference by states play an interactive role" (Chase-Dunn, 1977, pg. 455). In other words, "in the modern world-system there is only one mode of production, commodity production for profit on the world market, that articulates different forms of labor exploitation and encompasses a system of differentially powerful [(core)] states and peripheral areas" (Chase-Dunn, 1977, pg. 455) from whom concessions are extracted and social relations are normalized, regardless of race, ethnicity, gender, and sexuality, to meet the ends (profit-motive) of the capitalist system as driven by one powerful core state, the hegemon, and its national bourgeoisie—in today's global setting the US being that hegemon.

These two sociopolitical understandings regarding the origins and nature of globalization or the contemporary capitalist world-system under American hegemony, as Kevin Archer et al (2007) points out, have "set off a vigorous and at times rancorous debate within the social sciences (2007, pg. 2). On one side of the debate you have theorists who argue along the lines of the world-system view, and emphasize the "culture of globalization," the idea that "the constitutive role of culture is critical for grasping the continued hegemony of capitalism in the form of globalization…Culture, they assert is increasingly being co-opted and deployed as a new accumulation strategy to broaden and deepen the frontiers of capitalism and to displace its inherent crisis tendencies in core or postindustrial societies (Archer, 2007, pgs. 2-3). In a word, the cultures of the world and their material productions are commodified by the upper class of owners and high-level executives, operating in postindustrial world or core cities, to make a profit or produce surplus-value given the declining significance of profit from their investment in industrial production, which have been outsourced to Russia, China, Brazil, Mexico, India, and South Africa (BRICS nations) who have come to constitute the semi-periphery (industrial) nations of the capitalist world-system. Africa, the Caribbean, and some parts of Southeast Asia remain periphery (pre-industrial), i.e., agricultural and tourist states with some light manufacturing (baseballs, textiles, etc.) (Klak, 1998).

On the other side of the debate are those theorists who highlight "globalization-as-culture." They believe "that globalization is marked by the hollowing out of national cultural spaces either consequent upon the retrenchment of the nation state or because culture continues to be a relatively autonomous sphere" (Archer et al, 2007, pg. 2). That is, "[f]or the "globalization-as-culture" group…culture is not that easily enjoined due to its inherent counter-hegemonic properties vis-à-vis neo-liberal globalization. Rather, for this group…, contemporary globalization is not merely economic, but a system of multiple cultural articulations which are shaped by disjunctive space-time coordinates. In other words, globalization is as much if not more the product of inexorable and accelerated migratory cultural flows and electronic mass mediations beyond the space-time envelopes of the nation-state system and the successive socio-spatial fixes of global capitalism" (Archer et al, 2007, pg. 4). In fact, culture, in many instances, serves as a counter-hegemonic movement to (neo) liberal capitalism as a governing "rational" system.

THEORY AND METHOD

Theoretically, this debate between the advocates of the "culture-of-globalization" and the "culture-as-globalization" hypotheses is a fruitless debate grounded in a false ontological and epistemological understanding of the origins and nature of the (neo) liberal capitalist system that gives rise to the processes of the global relations of production, globalization, under American hegemony beginning in the 1970s. As Paul C. Mocombe (2012) highlights, both groups ontologically and epistemologically assume that the origins of capitalism and its discursive practice is grounded in reason and rationality, thus drawing on the liberal distinction between capitalism as a public and neutral system of rationality or rational rules of laws that stand apart from the understanding of it as a private sphere or lifeworld cultural form grounded in the ontology and epistemology of subjects/agents of the Protestant ethic and the spirit of capitalism. The latter Mocombeian/Weberian position, if assumed by both schools, we seek to argue here, is a point of convergence that resolves their opposition, and gives a better understanding to three things: first, the origins and nature of the processes of globalization; second, the nature of socialization of cultural groups within globalizing, i.e., neoliberal, processes; and third how African-Americans within this process are homogenizing or converging the black diaspora into their structurally differentiated (racial-class) social class language games produced by the aforementioned processes given their positions of power and visibility within the hegemon (US) of the capitalist world-system.

The intent of this work is to do just that, offer a rereading of globalization, based on a Mocombeian/Weberian metaphysical logic of social integration as outlined in *The Protestant Ethic and the Spirit of Capitalism*, of its development and processes. This is done for two reasons; first, to resolve the false positions of both (culture of globalization and globalization as culture) schools of thought; and second, to better understand the convergence thesis presented here that globally the black other in America and the diaspora is interpellated, integrated, and socialized or embourgeoised in the age of globalization within the racial-class dialectical dynamics and processes of black America represented by black underclass criminals, hip-hopsters, athletes, and entertainers on the one hand; and middle-class managers, entrepreneurs, educators, and preachers, on the other, as the bearers of ideological and linguistic domination for black folks in the capitalist world-system under American hegemony.

Essentially, our argument here, building on Paul C. Mocombe's (2012, 2014, 2015) structural Marxist work, is that both globalization schools of thought are putting forth the same convergence argument, the "culture of globalization" position from a Marxian systems integration perspective and the "globalization as culture" position from a Weberian social integration perspective. For the "culture of globalization" position cultural practices are homogenized so as to be integrated within the systemicity of capitalist relations of production and consumption at the world-system level so as to generate surplus-value from postindustrial (cultural products and entertainment), industrial, and or agricultural production. That is, each country, nation-state, or culture, has an economic role to play in the global capitalist world-system. That role, agricultural or industrial, is determined by the upper-class of owners and high level executives of corporations located predominantly in the US and other core or developed postindustrial nations who in-turn service the financial and (cultural) entertainment needs of the middle-classes of the world or nation-states, which they recreate, as an hybrid administrative bourgeoisie (comprador bourgeoisie, Frantz Fanon's term), through the outsourcing of work. The tastes and desires of this hybrid middle-class, initially (for black folks) created during slavery and colonialism given their interpellation and embourgeoisement via the mode of production and ideological apparatuses such as education, the media, the World Bank, UN, IMF, etc., are a direct parallel to the tastes and desires of the upper-class of owners and high-level executives. Hence via economic globalizing forces cultures are converged and homogenized via hybridization and the "retrenchment of the nation state' to participate in the global capitalist world-system as a multiethnic, multicultural, multiracial, etc. embourgeoised *other* seeking equality of opportunity, recognition, and distribution with their white counterparts against the material conditions of a multiethnic, multicultural, multiracial, etc., structurally differentiated, poor working and underclasses the world over working as laborers and cultural producers for postindustrial, core, markets, tourism, cheap call-center service workers or industrial workers in semi-periphery nations, and agricultural workers in periphery nations.

The globalization-as-cultural group suggests that in the process of acculturating social actors of nation-states to the organization of their work within the capitalist world-system, convergence and homogenization do not take place. Instead, in the process of integration within the world-system, cultural groups intersubjectively defer meaning in ego-centered communicative discourse to hybridize the lexicons of significations coming out of the globalization process thereby maintaining their cultural forms not in a commodified form but as a class-for-itself seeking to partake in the global community as hybrid social actors governed by the (neo) liberal rational logic of the marketplace.

The two positions are not mutually exclusive, however, and within a structural Marxist and Weberian logic of social integration apropos capitalist processes via mode of production, language, communicative discourse, ideology, and ideological apparatuses highlight the same position. Globalization, via American (neoliberal) hegemony, contemporarily represents the convergence and homogenization of social discourse and action via hybridization, which is tantamount to homogenization, and the "retrenchment of the nation state." That is globalization represents the discursive practice, "spirit of capitalism," of agents of the Protestant Ethic seeking to structuralize and homogenize, i.e., converge, through the mode of production and ideological apparatuses (church, prisons, the streets, police force, education, laws, World bank, IMF, WTO, etc.), outsourcing, mass mediaization, and consumption, "other" human behaviors, cultures, around the globe within the logic of their metaphysical discourse, "The Protestant Ethic and the spirit of capitalism," so as to accumulate profit, via agricultural, industrial, and post-industrial/consumerist production, for the predestined from the damned at the global level. In other words, via globalization social actors around the globe are interpellated, embourgeoised, and differentiated via their modes of production and state ideological apparatuses such as education, the media, and neoliberal market forces, funded by global ideological apparatuses, the IMF, World Bank, and United Nations (UN), via the US nation-state, to become agents of the Protestant ethic so as to fulfill their labor, production, and consumptive roles in the organization of work required by their nation-state in the global capitalist world-system under American hegemony. Integration and economic differentiation via the retrenchment of the nation state under American global hegemony subsequently leads to economic gain, upward mobility, and status for a few predestined, administrative bourgeoisie, or "transnational capitalist class" (Leslie Sklair's term), that in-turn become consumers, given the mediaization of society, of bourgeois goods and services from postindustrial (core) societies (the United States, Western Europe, Australia, and Japan). Conversely, the masses come to constitute a working and underclass, concentrated in rural communities and their capital cities (urban slums), producing cultural commodities and seeking work in their prescribed capital determining mode of production (agricultural, industrial, or postindustrial, i.e., low-end service jobs in tourism for example). Hence, proper socialization of the other in the contemporary capitalist American dominated world-system is tantamount to hybridization, i.e., the socialization of the other as a liberal/conservative bourgeois Protestant other (underclass or middle class, i.e., castes in classes) seeking equality of opportunity, recognition, and distribution with their white and administrative black bourgeois counterparts within the neoliberal framework of the global capitalist nation-state world-system under American hegemony at the expense of the masses who are laborers and cultural producers for tourists.

This process of convergence via hybridization is the legacy or by-product of the black American civil rights movement, led by a liberal hybrid embourgeoised middle class, on global corporate capital under American hegemony.

Under American global hegemony, hybridization (castes-in-classes) is not counter-hegemonic to globalizing capitalist processes; it is the mechanism of social integration and convergence in globalization. American capital, given their historical experience with the liberal hybrid black Americans' call and purposive-rationality for equality of opportunity, distribution, and recognition during the civil rights movement, learned that the desire of the hybrid is not to overthrow the capitalist system; instead, the embourgeoised liberal hybrid simply desires equality of opportunity, recognition, and distribution within the capitalist social structure (Fraser, 1994). Be that as it may, hybridization of other cultures, via the homogenization process of globalization, became the *modus operandi* of American global capital following the civil rights movement of the 1960s and adoption of civil rights legislation.

American capital beginning in the 1970s sought to outsource work to other nation-states in order to escape the high cost of labor and environmental laws in the US following the Roosevelt New Deal Era. Given the new civil rights legislations enacted in the 1960s to reinforce the American liberal bourgeois Protestant social order without regards to race, creed, nationality, etc. That discourse coupled with the discursive practice of outsourcing would be exported to other nation-states. American capital, therefore, sought to hybridized other ethnic cultures (turn them into castes in class) the world over via the organization of work and the retrenchment of the nation state in order to make social actors of other cultures known for two reasons, to socialize them to the work ethic of the neoliberal globalizing process and to accumulate surplus-value as American capital sought to service the others of their community as agents of and for capital, i.e., consumers and administrative bourgeoisie controlling production for global capital, in their emerging postindustrial (neoliberal) economy.

Consequently, given the ideological and material intent and influence of American capitalist lifestyles and practices in globalization coupled with the presence of black Americans in this process, the black diaspora, given they were already structurally differentiated along the same racial-class lines of black America following slavery, colonialism, and decolonization, became interpellated and embourgeoised or hybridized within the amalgamated racial-class dialectic of black America. This African-Americanization of the black diaspora via the class dialectic of black America is taking place by three means: 1) globalization or globalizing processes; 2) immigration to, and (convict) deportation from, the US by blacks from the diaspora; 3) and the influence of the global media industrial complex in diasporic or African nation-states.

DISCUSSION

In the age of neoliberal globalization or the contemporary capitalist world-system under American hegemony, the discourse and discursive practices of the black bourgeoisies, working and underclasses around the world, i.e., Africa and the black diaspora, are ever-so slowly becoming African-Americanized via 1) globalizing economic processes; 2) their integration into the class dynamics and processes of black America via immigration to, and deportation from, the US; and 3) because of the material influence of the Protestant ethic and the spirit of capitalism promulgated throughout the diaspora by the power elites of the black underclass (Hip-Hop culture), criminals, rappers, athletes, entertainers, and street personalities; and black American charismatic liberal bourgeois Protestant preachers like TD Jakes, Creflo Dollar, Juanita Bynum, Eddie Long, etc. who, given their material wealth, have become the bearers of ideological and linguistic domination in black America, and are seeking to do the same in Africa and the black diaspora. Just as in black America, globalization or globalizing economic processes under American hegemony reinforced and reproduced the two structurally differentiated social class language games in the nation-states of Africa and the black diaspora from slavery, colonialism, and decolonization: a black administrative bourgeoisie and working/underclass of urban and rural dwellers looking either for work in the cities or to immigrate to the US and elsewhere, former Metropoles of the diaspora, for work and better economic opportunities.

Post-WWII neoliberal policies prescribed by the IMF, World Bank, United Nations, etc., forced black countries in the Caribbean and Africa to adopt structural adjustment policies and modes of production, i.e., agribusiness, manufacturing, tourism, and athletics, which drove the citizenry from rural areas into cities looking for work in outsourced factories, tourism, or call centers for multinational corporations. Those who were able to find employment in the cities became a part of the working class modeling the lifestyles of government officials and middle managers (the administrative bourgeoisies of colonialism) who served as an administrative bourgeoisie for global capital. Contrarily, those who were unable to find employment looked either to immigrate elsewhere or to criminal activities to sustain themselves. Whereas the organization of work, church, and education became the dominant ideological apparatuses for the interpellation and embourgeoisement of the working class and administrative bourgeoisie; the entertainment and athletic industries, streets, and prisons became the dominant ideological apparatuses for the unemployed youth who came to constitute an urban underclass in the slums of these societies.

As such, in the globalizing process under American hegemony, the black administrative bourgeoisies, working and underclasses of the black diaspora would come to fall within the racial-class dialectic of black America. On the one hand, the former two are influenced by the language and ideology of black American charismatic liberal bourgeois Protestant preachers in the likes of TD Jakes, Creflo Dollar, Eddie Long, and Juanita Bynum whose prosperity gospel permeates throughout the black Protestant churches of the diaspora. On the other hand, the black poor youth (underclasses) of the cities of the diaspora are influenced by black American (amalgamated) underclass language and ideology represented in the language and ideology of criminals, street personalities, black rappers, entertainers, and athletes whose images, along with their bourgeois counterparts, are overrepresented in the media. Blacks in the diaspora are further influenced by the class dynamics and social relations of production of black America when structural global forces drive them to immigrate to the US in search of economic opportunities in urban communities where work has disappeared to the suburbs and semi-periphery nations, China, South Africa, Brazil, Mexico, and India, or when they visit and or are deported back to their nation-states for criminal offenses committed in the US. The children of black migrants from the diaspora overtime become integrated within the aforementioned social class language games of black America via its ideological apparatuses, i.e., the black church, education, the streets, prisons, and athletic and entertainment industries. They add admixtures of their own underclass practices to the latter, and transmit their inherited amalgamated practical consciousnesses back to the black diaspora via their visit or deportation. Conversely, the adults, in the ideological apparatuses (churches predominantly) of their ethnic communities, pattern their lifestyles after the black American and bourgeoisie classes of their home country under the leadership of educated black professionals and preachers influenced by their American counterparts whose underclass they hold in contempt.

So the logic here is that, as many globalization theorists of the postmodernist variety have demonstrated (Bell, 1976; Harvey, 1989; Giddens, 1990; Jameson, 1991; Arrighi, 1994; Sklair, 2001; Kellner, 2001; Mocombe, 2012), contemporary (1970 to the present) economic conditions in America are no longer characterized or driven by the industrial means for accumulating capital, which dominated the social relations of production of the last one hundred years. Instead, the present globalization condition is driven-by, post-industrialism (consumerism)—the new means for accumulating capital—, and in such "developed" societies like the U.S., is characterized not by the industrial organization of labor, but rather by capitalist service occupations catering to the consumerist (financial and entertainment) demands of a dwindling (transnational) middle class.

The rate of economic gain for its own sake or profit has fallen in industrial production due to labor laws and ecological cost in developed postindustrial countries like the US; hence the practice now among investors operating out of the US is on financial expansion "in which 'over-accumulated' capital switches from investments in production and trade, to investments in finance, property titles, and other claims on future income" (Trichur, 2005, pg. 165). Globally, the economic bifurcation defining this current conjuncture is characterized, on the one hand, by an expansion or outsourcing of industrial production into developing or periphery and semi-periphery countries (China, Brazil, Mexico, India, and South Africa), where the rate of labor exploitation has risen given their lack of labor laws; and, on the other hand, consumerism of cheaply produced goods and high-end service occupations have come to dominate (postindustrial) developed societies (US, Western Europe, Japan, and Australia).

Be that as it may, economically and socially, the major emphasis among governing elites in this US dominated global economy or social relation of production has been participation or integration of cultural "others" (specifically "hybrids") into the existing configuration of (neoliberal) power relations, as a racial-caste-in-class, in order to accumulate profits by servicing the diverse financial wants and entertainment needs of commodified cultural groups, throughout the globe. A select few (Leslie Sklair's transnational capitalist class) live a "bourgeois" middle and upper middle class lifestyle at the expense of the masses working in low-wage agricultural, manufacturing, and cultural productive jobs or not at all given the transfer of these jobs overseas to lesser developing countries.

American blacks, as interpellated (workers) and embourgeoised agents of the American postindustrial capitalist social structure of inequality, represent the most modern (i.e. socialized) people of color, in terms of their "practical consciousness," in this process of homogenizing social actors as agents of the protestant ethic or disciplined workers, producers, and consumers working for owners of production in order to obtain economic gain, status, and upward mobility in the larger American society (Frazier, 1957; Wilson, 1978; Glazer and Moynihan, 1963; Mocombe, 2009). They constitute the American social space in terms of their relation to the means of production in post-industrial capitalist (and its ideological apparatuses) America, which differentiates black America for the most part into two status groups or social class language games, a dwindling middle and upper class (living in suburbia) that numbers about 25 percent of their population (13 percent) and obtain their status as doctors, athletes, entertainers, lawyers, teachers, and other high-end professional service occupations; and a growing segregated "black underclass" of unemployed and under-employed wage-earners, gangsters, rappers, athletes, and cultural producers occupying poor inner-city communities and schools focused solely on technical skills, multicultural education, athletics, and test-taking for social promotion given the relocation (outsourcing) of industrial and manufacturing jobs to poor periphery and semi-periphery countries and the introduction of low-end post-industrial service jobs and a growing informal economy in American urban-cities. Consequently, the poor performance of black American students, vis-à-vis whites, in education as an ideological apparatus for this post-industrial capitalist sociolinguistic worldview leaves them disproportionately in this growing underclass of laborers, rappers, gangsters, criminals, athletes, and entertainers at the bottom of the American postindustrial racial-class social structure of inequality unable to either transform their world as they encounter it, or truly exercise their embourgeoisement given their lack of, what sociologist Pierre Bourdieu (1973, 1984) refers to as, capital (cultural, social, economic, and political).

Ironically, contrary to John Ogbu's (1986) burden of acting white hypothesis, it is due to their indigent (pathological-pathogenic) structural position within the American capitalist social structure of inequality, as opposed to a differing or oppositional cultural ethos from that of the latter, as to the reason why many black American school children underachieve vis-à-vis their white counterparts. That is, the majority of black American school students underachieve in school in general and on standardized test in particular, vis-à-vis their white counterparts, not because they possess or are taught (by their peers) at an early age distinct normative cultural values from that of the dominant group of owners and high-level executives in the social structure that transfer into cultural and political conflict in the classroom as an ideological apparatus for capitalists. To the contrary, black American students underachieve in school because in acquiring the "verbal behavior" of the dominant powers of the social structure in segregated "poor" gentrified inner-city communities which lack good legal jobs and affordable resources that have been outsourced by capital overseas (outsourcing), the majority, who happen to be less educated in the "Standard English" of the society, have reinforced a linguistic (Black English Vernacular) community or status group of hustlers, rappers, athletes, and entertainers, the black underclass, as the bearers of ideological and linguistic domination for black America, which have been commodified by finance capital to accumulate surplus-value in their postindustrial economy (Mocombe, 2006, 2011; Mocombe and Tomlin, 2010, 2013).

It is this "mismatch of linguistic social class function," role conflict, the ideals of middle class black and white bourgeois America against the perceived "pathologies" (functions) of the black underclass as a sociolinguistic status group in the American postindustrial class social structure of inequality, Ogbu and other post-segregationist black middle-class scholars inappropriately label, "acting-white," "culture of poverty," or oppositional culture. Blacks are not concealing their academic prowess and abilities when they focus, and defer their efforts, on hustling, athletics, music, entertainment, etc. for fear of acting white as Ogbu suggests. They are focusing on racially coded socioeconomic actions or roles reified and commodified in the larger American postindustrial capitalist social structure of inequality that are more likely to lead to economic gain, status, prestige, and upward mobility in the society as defined for, and by, the black underclass financed by finance capital.

The black underclass youth in America's ghettoes have slowly become, since the 1980s, with the financialization of hip-hop culture by record labels such as Sony and others, athletics, and the entertainment industry, the bearers of ideological and linguistic domination for the black (youth) community in America. Their language and worldview as constituted through hip-hop culture, athletics and the entertainment industries financed by white finance capital, has, decentered the subject of the black bourgeoisie, and become the means by which many black youth (and youth throughout the world) attempt to recursively reorganize and reproduce their material resource framework against the purposive-rationality of black bourgeois or middle class America. The upper-class of owners and high-level executives of the American dominated capitalist world-system have capitalized on this through the commodification of black underclass street, criminal, athletic, and entertainment culture. This is further supported by an American media and popular culture that glorifies athletes, entertainers, and the "Bling bling," wealth, diamonds, cars, jewelry, and money. Hence the aim of many young black people, black males in particular, in the society is no longer to seek status, economic gain, and upward mobility through a Protestant Ethic that stresses hard work, diligence, differed gratification, and education; on the contrary, sports, music, instant gratification, illegal activities (drug dealing), and skimming are the dominant means portrayed for their efforts through the athletic and entertainment industries financed by post-industrial capital. Schools throughout urban American inner cities are no longer seen as means to a professional end in order to obtain economic gain, status, and upward mobility, but obstacles to that end because it delays gratification and is not correlative with the means, social roles, associated with economic success, status, and upward mobility in black urban America. More black American youth (especially the black male) want to become, football and basketball players, rappers and entertainers, like many of their role models who were raised in their underclass environments and obtained economic gain and upward mobility that way, over doctors, lawyers, engineers, etc., the social functions associated with the status symbol of the black and white middle professional (educated) class of the civil rights generation. Hence the end and social action remains the same, economic success, status, and upward economic mobility, only the means to that end have shifted with the rise, financed by finance capital, of the black underclass as the bearers of ideological and linguistic domination in black America given the commodification of so-called hip-hop culture and their high visibility in the media and charitable works through basketball and football camps and rap concerts, which reinforce the aforementioned activities as viable means to wealth, upward mobility, and status in the society's postindustrial economy, which focuses on services and entertainment for the world's transnational bourgeois class as the mode of producing surplus-value.

This linguistic and ideological domination and the ends of the power elites (rappers, athletes, gangsters, hustlers, etc.) of the black underclass, "mismatch of linguistic structure and social function," which brings about the role conflict Ogbu interprets as the burden of acting white, are juxtaposed against the Protestant Ethic and spirit of capitalism of the black middle and upper middle educated professional classes represented in the prosperity discourse and discursive practices of black American preachers and professionals in the likes of Michael Eric Dyson, TD Jakes, Creflo Dollar, Eddie Long, Juanita Bynum, etc. who push forth, via the black American church, education and professional jobs as viable means to prosperity, status, and upward economic gain in the society. Hence, whereas, for agents of the Protestant Ethic and the spirit of capitalism in the likes of Dyson, Jakes, Dollar, Bynum, and Eddie Long the means to "Bling bling," or the American Dream, is through education, obtaining a professional job, and material wealth as a sign of God's grace, salvation, and blessings; Rapping, hustling, sports, etc., for younger black Americans growing up in gentrified inner-cities throughout the US, where industrial work has disappeared, represent the means (not education) to the status position of "Bling bling." So what we are suggesting here, building on the work of Mocombe (2012, 2013, 2014, 2015, 2016), is that contemporarily many black American youth are not "acting white" when education no longer becomes a priority or the means to economic gain, status, and upward mobility, as they get older and consistently underachieve vis-à-vis whites; they are attempting to be white and achieve bourgeois economic status (the "Bling bling" of cars, diamonds, gold, helicopters, money, etc.) in the society by being "black," speaking Ebonics, rapping, playing sports, hustling, etc., in a racialized post-industrial capitalist social structure wherein the economic status of "blackness" is (over) determined by the white capitalists class of owners and high-level executives and the black proletariats of the West, the black underclass, whose way of life and image ("athletes, hustlers, hip-hopsters") has been commodified (by white and black capitalists) and distributed throughout the world for entertainment, (black) status, and economic purposes in post-industrial capitalist America. This amalgamated (there are cross-cultural influences between black American and diasporic groups, i.e., rap and hip-hop culture emerges as a cross between black American/Haitian jazz, blues, and Jamaican dance hall music) underclass practical consciousness is globally promulgated to urban black youth (who share the same structural positions in their home countries to that of the black Americans) throughout the black diaspora by finance capital via Black Entertainment Television (BET) and other media outlets, and is counterbalanced or opposed by black preachers promoting the same ethos, The Protestant Ethic and the spirit of capitalism, via the prosperity gospel, patriarchy, misogyny, etc., of the black American churches, to the black administrative bourgeoisie and working classes (who share their structural positions) around the world via biblical conversion or salvation, over the so-called pathologies, promiscuity, misogyny, patriarchy, etc., of the underclasses, as the medium to and for success in the capitalist world-system. Hence, the social structure of class (not racial or cultural worldview) inequality that characterizes the black American social environment is subsequently the class division and relational framework, which black youth and the black administrative bourgeoisie in the diaspora are exposed to and socialized in when they encounter globalizing processes (globalization) through immigration to, or (convict) deportation from, the US, the outsourcing of work from America, and the images of the athletic and entertainment industries and the black church.

CONCLUSIONS

Throughout the continent of Africa, the Caribbean, and black Europe black American charismatic preachers are promoting a prosperity gospel (economic gain for its own sake and material wealth as a sign of God's grace and blessings) among the black poor and administrative bourgeoisie, which is usually juxtaposed against the emergence of an underclass practical consciousness among the youth in these areas influenced by the criminality, hip-hop, and athletic culture or social class language game of the black American underclass (Ntarangwi, 2009). Nigerian, South African, East African, St. Lucian, Jamaican, Haitian, and black British Caribbean Hip-Hop, gangsta rap music, Bling bling, dress code, etc., influenced by the black American underclass are juxtaposed against the Protestant evangelism of Nigerian, South African, East African, St. Lucian, Jamaican, Haitian, and black British Caribbean preachers and gospel artists influenced by TD Jakes, Creflo Dollar, Juanita Bynum, and other black charismatic preachers and gospel artists whose global outreach throughout the diaspora are converting other blacks to agents of the Protestant Ethic and the spirit of capitalism via their prosperity gospel.

These two structural differentiated racial-class identities, which emerge out of slavery, colonialism, decolonization, and postindustrial America, the hegemon of globalization, represent the racial-class (caste) dynamics within which black others throughout the world are dialectically interpellated, integrated, and embourgeoised into the capitalist world-system. Contemporarily, as blacks in the diaspora are displaced from rural areas to urban ones in their home countries and immigration to the US and elsewhere (the Metropoles of the former colonies) as a result of neoliberal policies of the IMF, World Bank, and United Nations under American hegemony, their societies come to be structured by the practical consciousness, ideology, and ideological apparatuses of black American society. Black youth and adults come into contact with the black American practical consciousness of the black underclass and bourgeoisie via church conferences, gospel and rap concerts, basketball and football camps, the organization of work, BET, and other media outlets, which promulgate the amalgamated work ethic, church, athletic, entertainment, criminal, and street culture of black America to the diaspora. These converging processes are undergirded by the images, ideologies, ideological apparatuses of black American preachers, athletes, entertainers, etc. in America and the diaspora who come to serve as role models for other blacks in the Protestant capitalist world-system. The black administrative bourgeoisie and working classes, given their interpellation and embourgeoisement in their home countries via the organization of work, church, and education, come to pattern their practical consciousness around the black American bourgeoisie and working classes under the leadership of preachers, gospel artists, and educated professionals, which have supplanted the white colonial slavemasters. Conversely, black youth in the diaspora come to pattern themselves around the practical consciousness of the black American underclass given their interpellation and embourgeoisement, like their black American counterparts, via the lack of work, streets, prisons, and athletic and entertainment industries in their home countries and the US. As a result, black diasporic identities is divided between a black administrative bourgeoisie and working classes with black preachers and educated professionals as leaders and social role models, and an underclass youth presence influenced by the streets, criminal, and athletic and entertainment industries of their native countries and black America whose practical consciousness is amalgamated as a result of the presence of diasporic identities amongst its representatives. Hence whereas the former seeks economic gain, status, and upward mobility through education; the latter, in patterning the underclass dynamics of black America, does so through criminal activities, athletics, and the commodification of their musical genres, culinary tastes, and adoption of so-called black American hip-hop culture (with an ethnic twist) to sell to tourists in their home countries and abroad. The intent of this work is to explore how it is that black America emerged as the bearers of ideological and linguistic domination for Africa and the African diaspora through what we are calling the African-Americanization of the black diaspora.

To begin this analysis, chapter one deconstructs contemporary postmodern/post-structural understandings regarding the nature and origins of black American identity/practical consciousness. Against postmodern/post-structural emphasis on the fragmentary or the decentered subject, this work, using a structural Marxist perspective grounded in structuration theory, chapter two, suggests that the constitution of black practical consciousness/identity must be understood predominantly as the by-product of Protestant capitalist racial-class divisions, social relations of production, and ideological apparatuses. Be that as it may, chapter three highlights the nature and origins of globalization under American hegemony within a structurationist framework. Suggesting that following World War II, globalization emerges as a product of the discourse of the Protestant Ethic and the discursive practices of the spirit of capitalism embedded in neoliberal policies under American corporate hegemony. Chapter four explores the origins and constitution of black American identity/practical consciousness within the dialectic of the discourse of the Protestant Ethic and the discursive practices of the spirit of capitalism. Concluding, in this structural approach to the constitution of black American practical consciousness, that in the historical denouement of the Protestant Ethic and the discursive practices of the spirit of capitalism from slavery to globalization and America's postindustrial economy black American consciousness became dominated for the most part by two social class language games, that of the black underclass and that of the black bourgeois professional class, which discriminated against all other modes of being-in-the world arrived-at through the deferment of meaning in ego-centered communicative discourse; the drives of the body; and impulses of subatomic particles.

Chapter five discusses how historically the aforementioned two social class language games emerged in Africa, the Caribbean, and the United Kingdom (UK). The chapter concludes the work by highlighting the impacts the African-Americanization of black people in the diaspora have in developing a global black identity that perpetuates their proletarianization, academic underachievement, exploitation, and oppression.

Chapter One

Black Consciousnesses and Identities in America and the Diaspora

From slavery, to colonialism, to the present, race and class distinctions within black communities in the United States (US) and the black diaspora must be understood as being predominantly constituted within and by the two dominant social class language games, a black bourgeoisie and underclass (a racial caste in class), created by the racial-class division and social relations of production of global capitalism or the capitalist world-system and its ideological apparatuses. This structural Marxist dialectical perspective, we are purporting, stands against contemporary postcolonial, postmodern, and post-structural theories, which focus on local formations, heterogeneity, the diverse, the subjective, the spontaneous, the relative, and the fragmentary as the basis for understanding the constitution of black identities and consciousnesses in the US and the diaspora in the age of globalization. The latter positions, we argue here, are also the product of class division and social relations of production in late postindustrial capitalist development and organization. The concepts, i.e., ambivalence, double consciousness, hybridity, négritude, créolité, and intersectionality, coming from these theories represent the concepts, psychological pathologies, and practical consciousnesses of the black bourgeoisies and other bourgeoisies of once discriminated against others in their quest to obtain equality of opportunity, recognition, and distribution with their former slavemasters and colonial administrators. As a result, they fail to adequately address the issues regarding the origins and basis for the constitution of black identities and consciousnesses in America, the Metropoles, and the diaspora. Using a variant of structuration theory, what Paul C. Mocombe (2014, 2015, 2016) calls phenomenological structuralism, this work, against contemporary postcolonial, postmodern, and post-structural theories, seeks to offer a dialectical understanding of the constitution of black American and diasporic lives within the class division and social relations of production of the global capitalist world-system (and its ideological apparatuses), while accounting for black social agency. In the end, we utilize Mocombe's phenomenological structuralism to explore the African-Americanization of the black diaspora hypothesis as an explanatory framework for understanding the constitution of black identity in America and the diaspora in the age of neoliberal globalization or the contemporary capitalist world-system under American neoliberal hegemony.

Since the 1960s, there have been four similar schools of thought on understanding the origins and nature of black practical consciousnesses, the ideas blacks recursively reorganize and reproduce in their material practices, in the United States (US), the United Kingdom (UK), and the diaspora: the pathological-pathogenic and adaptive-vitality school in the US; and the anti-essentialist and anti-anti-essentialist schools in the UK and the diaspora. In the US, the pathological-pathogenic position suggests that in its divergences from white American norms and values black American practical consciousness is nothing more than a pathological form of, and reaction to, American consciousness rather than a dual (both African and American) hegemonic opposing "identity-in-differential" (the term is Gayatri Spivak's) to the American one (Elkins, 1959; Frazier, 1939,1957; Genovese, 1974; Murray, 1984; Moynihan, 1965; Myrdal, 1944; Wilson, 1978, 1987; Sowell, 1975, 1981; Stampp, 1956, 1971). Proponents of the adaptive-vitality school suggest that the divergences are not pathologies but African "institutional transformations" preserved on the American landscape (Allen, 2001; Asante, 1988, 1990; Billingsley, 1968, 1970, 1993; Blassingame, 1972; Early, 1993; Gilroy, 1993; Gutman, 1976; Herskovits, 1958 [1941]; Holloway, 1990a; Karenga, 1993; Levine, 1977; Lewis, 1993; Lincoln and Mamiya, 1990; Nobles, 1987; Staples, 1978; Stack, 1974; West, 1993). Just the same in the UK and the diaspora, the two main opposing schools of thought are the anti-essentialist and the anti-anti-essentialist (Smith, 1960; Vera, 1960; Gilroy, 1993; Mercer, 1994; Clifford, 1997; Mocombe and Tomlin, 2010, 2013; Mocombe et al, 2014). Anti-essentialists as in the case of the US pathological-pathogenic school argue against any ideas of a black innate cultural phenomenon that unites all black people, and contends that diasporic identities and cultures cannot place African origin at the center of any attempt to understand the nature of black practical consciousnesses in the UK and the diaspora (Mercer, 1994, pg. 3). The anti-anti-essentialist position, in keeping with the logic of the adaptive-vitality school, posits, on the contrary, the idea that African memory retentions exist in diasporic cultures to some degree (Clifford, 1997, pg. 267-268). Contemporarily, all four positions have been criticized for either their structural determinism as in the case of the pathological-pathogenic and anti-essentialist approaches, or racial/cultural determinism as in the case of the adaptive-vitality and anti-anti-essentialist positions (Karenga, 1993; Mocombe et al, 2014).

In directly or indirectly refuting these four positions for their structural and racial/cultural determinism, contemporary post-sixties and post-segregation era black scholars in the United Kingdom (UK) and United States (US) attempt to understand black consciousnesses and communities by using post-colonial, post-structural, and post-modern theories to either reinterpret W.E.B. Du Bois's (1903) double consciousness construct as an epistemological mode of critical inquiry that characterizes the nature or essence of black consciousness, a la Cornel West (1993) and Paul Gilroy (1993); or, building on the social constructivist work of Frantz Fanon, offer an intersectional approach to the constitution of black consciousnesses and communities, which emphasizes the diverse and different levels of alienation, marginalization, and domination, class, race, gender, global location, age, and sexual identity, by which black consciousnesses and communities get constituted, a la bell hooks (1993) and Patricia Hill Collins (1990) (Reed, 1997; Gordon, 2000; Mocombe et al, 2014). In spite of their efforts, these two dominant contemporary critical race theory responses to the pathological-pathogenic, adaptive-vitality, anti-essentialist, and anti-anti-essentialist positions inadequately resolve the structural and racial determinism of the aforementioned approaches by neglecting the fact that their theories and the practical consciousness of the theorists themselves derive from the class division and social relations of production of global capitalism or the contemporary capitalist world-system (Mocombe et al, 2014).

The former understanding, Du Boisian double consciousness, put forth by Paul Gilroy and Cornel West is not only problematic because it reiterates Du Bois's racial essentialism in constituting his notion of double consciousness (Reed, 1997; Mocombe, 2008). But the scholars are also mistaken because they assume their Cartesian, transcendental, intellectual activity, the epistemological mode of critical inquiry, in the academy as having ontological and epistemological status among the black masses in general in constituting their identity within and by the dialectical racial-class structure of global capitalist relations of production and its ideological apparatuses. In other words, instead of viewing their interpretation of Du Boisian double consciousness, as an epistemological mode of critical inquiry, as being a by-product of a Cartesian transcendental vantage point afforded to them by their academic training and bourgeois class positions as black professors seeking to define black consciousness along the social class language game of the white bourgeois lifestyles of the upper-class of owners and high-level executives as it stands against and in relation to black underclass bodies, material conditions, language, and ideology. Gilroy and West assume their interpretation of double consciousness as an epistemological mode of critical inquiry, which is similar to the negative dialectics of the Frankfurt School, to be how ontologically and epistemologically black people, whether in the US or the diaspora ("the black Atlantic"), in general come to constitute their practical consciousnesses within the modern state and the dialectic of the capitalist social structure of class inequality and differentiation of the West. In doing so, however, they neglect the fact that their conception, as was the case in W.E.B. Du Bois's conceptualization of double consciousness following the American Civil War, derives from the racial-class divisions of the American industrial/postindustrial capitalist social relations of production and its ideological apparatuses, which created two social (racial) class language games, a racial-caste-in-class, a black bourgeois educated and professional class juxtaposed against the material conditions, practices, language, body, and ideology of a black underclass segregated in the ghettoes of Northern cities where industrial work was beginning to disappear to developing countries following the end of World War II. West and Gilroy, as Du Bois attempted to do for Southern agricultural black Americans following the Civil War, use double consciousness to highlight the contradictions of the society as encapsulated in, and revealed by, the material conditions of the black underclass of Northern cities in order to seek equality of opportunity, recognition, and distribution for them vis-à-vis whites and black bourgeois material conditions, bodies, language, status, etc. in a declining industrial social relations of production (Fraser, 1994; Reed, 1997; Mocombe, 2008, 2009).

Just the same, the latter predominantly feminist position, conversely, in refutation to the assumed hidden logic of heterosexual and patriarchal domination inherent in the theories of Du Bois, Gilroy, and West, attempts to offer an intersectional approach to the constitution of black consciousnesses, which emphasizes the different levels of domination, class, race, gender, global location, age, and sexual identity, by which black communities and consciousnesses get alienated, marginalized, and constituted. This postcolonial, postmodern, post-structural, and black feminist theorizing of bell hooks and Patricia Hill Collins, especially, epistemologically dismisses the dominant ontological status of the capitalist system/social structure by which the masses of blacks attempt to practically live out their lives for the theoretical assumptions of the indeterminacy of meaning and decentered subject of postcolonial, post-structural, and post-modern theorizing. They attempt to read back into the historical constitution of black identity and community life within and by the dialectic of a global capitalist social structure of racial class inequality the indeterminacy of meaning and decentered subject of postcolonial, post-structural, and post-modern theorizing to highlight the variety of intersecting ways, race, class, age, sexual identity, etc., individual black subjects were and are alienated, marginalized, and dominated. As such, they commit the same bourgeois Cartesian transcendental intellectual fallacy that Gilroy and West do. Both hooks and Collins, from their transcendental vantage points, put the ontological status of the capitalist world-system, or "matrix of domination" to quote Collins, as reflected in the practices of the majority of blacks under erasure for the ontological and epistemological assumptions of postcolonial, post-modern, and post-structural theorizing. As though their bourgeois epistemological assumptions within a contemporary postindustrial capitalist social structure that attempts to decenter the bourgeois subject in order to reify and commodify individual identities around their class positions for capital accumulation, is how all blacks, historically, initially encountered the matrix of domination and came to constitute their being-in-the-world within and by the global capitalist social structure of racial class inequality and differentiation. They fail to realize that intersectionality is a socio-political by-product of a postindustrial capitalist landscape or social structure seeking to decenter the bourgeois subject and allow a diversity of identities to emerge (around their class positions) within the class division and social relations of postindustrial capitalist production so as to accumulate surplus-value by catering to the entertainment, financial, and service needs of these new and once discriminated-against identities and their constructed "fictitious" class-based communities.

Both positions because of their class origins and Cartesian ontological and epistemological (transcendental) activities and vantage points inadequately address the issue of how their intellectual assumptions and the practical consciousnesses in black communities within the global capitalist matrix of domination of the West historically and ontologically became constituted within and by the dialectical unfolding of racial-class divisions and social relations of production organized via mode of production, language, ideology, ideological apparatuses, and communicative discourse. They fail to synthesize their transcendental academic rhetoric with structural Marxist dialectics, which captures the racial-class divisions, ideological apparatuses, and the dialectical economic structure within which the practical consciousnesses of the black masses, the academic theories of ambivalence, hybridity, créolité, négritude, double consciousness, intersectionality, and the identities of the theorists emerged.

In other words, building on both the post-structural notion of the indeterminacy of meaning in ego-centered communicative discourse, i.e., linguistic communication and interaction is between endless signifiers and not signifiers and signified which allows for meaning to be deferred during interaction, as highlighted by Jacques Derrida; and the postmodern notion of the decentered subject, the rejection of the notion of individual subjectivity as autonomous, self-critical, unified, and stable, i.e., the transcendental subject of Kantian discourse, for the understanding of the subject as a locus of multiple, dispersed or decentered discourses, of Michel Foucault, bell hooks and Patricia Hill Collins, paradoxically from a transcendental academic perspective, offer an intersectional approach to the constitution of black consciousnesses and communities, which emphasizes the diverse and different levels of domination, class, race, gender, global location, age, and sexual identity, by which individual black consciousnesses and communities get constituted. Cornel West and Paul Gilroy in keeping with the logic of the transcendental subject of Kantian discourse offer Du Boisian double consciousness as an epistemological mode of critical inquiry into modernity as being the fundamental characteristic of black individual consciousness with a touch of religiosity and jazz improvisation. However, in doing so, like Derrida and Foucault, who neglect the fact that the indeterminacy of meaning and the decentered subject operate relationally within structures of domination, since the seventeenth century within the modern form of the state and racial-class divisions, which derives from the mode of production, language, communicative discourse, ideology, and ideological apparatuses of Protestant capitalist relations of production, West, Gilroy, hooks, and Collins overlook the fact that their theories and the different levels of domination they point to as constituting black communities and consciousnesses derive from the contemporary organization of the modern state and class division in postindustrial capitalist societies.

That is, the social phenomenon of Du Boisian double consciousness (adopted by West and Gilroy) and the indeterminacy of meaning and the decentered subject highlighted by Derrida and Foucault in the intersectionality language of hooks and Collins occur in relation to the state and its ideological apparatuses and racial-class divisions of *postindustrial* capitalist societies. They both have their basis in the relations of production, exploitation, and organization of the state following the failed diverse student revolutions of the 1960s, which gave rise to local formations and heterogeneity as the theoretical theme for the new philosophers and social scientists of the late twentieth century who sought equality of opportunity, recognition, and distribution for the diverse groups of the student movements within the class division and global social relations of capitalist production and organization, which became triumphant with the fall of communism or state capitalism in Eastern Europe (Fraser, 1994).

That is to say, the double consciousness and intersectionality discourses of Du Bois, West, Gilroy, hooks, and Collins have their basis in globalization and the postindustrial relations of production and exploitation as organized under the hegemony of the American nation-state following the civil rights and hippie movements of the 1960s, which diversified and fragmentized subjectivities and social movements for the philosophy of the person, individual human rights, and freedoms to (speak, assemble, etc.). Whereas Gilroy and West articulated their intellectual activities within the embourgeoisement and proletarianization of blacks during an industrial and an emerging postindustrial modernism and organization of the state that juxtaposed, like Du Bois, the bodies, language, and material conditions of an emerging black underclass, which moved to Northern urban ghettoes from the agricultural

South during the process of deindustrialization and suburbanization that saw industrial work transferred overseas, vis-à-vis the material conditions of a black bourgeois professional class working in professional high-end service occupations and the entertainment industry clamoring for equality of opportunity, recognition, and distribution for the former via education and redistribution of wealth by the welfare state. Both hooks and Collins, articulate their theories within a postindustrial capitalism that fosters identity politics for capital accumulation via financialization and cultural consumption. Hence, Du Bois, West, Gilroy, hooks, and Collins fail to realize that their identities and theories derive from the state and class division within the processes of globalization and postindustrial capitalist relations of production and its ideological apparatuses.

Put differently, the logic here is that the theories of West, Gilroy, hooks, and Collins regarding the constitution of black consciousnesses derive from the class division of neoliberal policies of globalizing capitalist processes under American hegemony and postindustrial capitalist relations of the nation-state and its ideological apparatuses. It is the class division and social relations of production coupled with the experience of white American capital with the liberal hybrid embourgeoised black American's struggle for equality of opportunity, recognition, and distribution beginning in slavery and ending in the civil rights movement of the 1960s, which led to the passage of civil rights legislation that integrated blacks into the fabric of the society under the purposive-rationality of their liberal black hybrid leadership in the likes of W.E.B. Du Bois, Martin Luther King Jr., Barack Obama, etc., which would come to constitute the contemporary processes of globalization and this adoption of postcolonial, postmodern, and post-structural theory highlighted in the works of Gilroy, West, hooks, and Collins, in other words.

Following the civil rights movement of the 1960s and adoption of civil rights legislation such as the Civil Rights Act of 1964, the experience of white American capital with embourgeoised liberal hybrid blacks would give rise to hybridization as the mechanism of social integration for all ethnic, racial, cultural, sexual, etc., minorities into American postindustrial capitalist relations of production locally and globally. Locally, discrimination was outlawed throughout American society and its ideological apparatuses, which in theory became a color-blind multicultural, multiracial, multisexual, etc., postindustrial social setting with emphasis on individual human rights and freedoms to, speak, assemble, etc., amidst class differentiation. Subsequently, the global outsourcing of industrial work by American capital beginning in the 1970s would be coupled with hybridization, individuality, human rights and *freedoms to* as the mechanisms of social integration for ethnic, racial, cultural, sexual, etc., others into global capitalist relations of production under American hegemony. That is, under the passage of civil rights legislation such as the Civil Rights Act of 1964 to integrate liberal hybrid blacks into the fabric of American society and its ideological apparatuses, the American nation-state reinforced its liberal/conservative bourgeois Protestantism without regards to race, creed, nationality, sex, religion, etc. With the advent of outsourcing or globalization under American hegemony beginning in the 1970s, other ethnic, racial, gender, and other minorities the world-over were integrated or socialized, like the liberal hybrid black Americans, via ideology and ideological apparatuses such as human rights, freedom, education, the streets, prisons, media, Protestant churches, World Bank, International Monetary Fund (IMF), etc., to work for American capital within the global framework of this color-blind new world economic order with its ideological emphasis on human rights and *freedoms to*. In the processes of globalization, American capital sought and seeks to hybridize other ethnic, cultural, sexual, and racial others the world over via the retrenchment of the nation state and color-blind neoliberal economic legislation in order to make social actors of other cultures known for two reasons, however: first, to socialize them to the work ethic of the globalizing capitalist relations of production; and second, to accumulate surplus-value as American capital sought and seeks to service the elite others of ethnic, racial, gender, and other communities as agents of and for capital, i.e., cultural producers, consumers, and administrative bourgeoisie controlling production for global capital, for their postindustrial economy. Conversely, the interpellated and embourgeoised hybridized ethnic, cultural, sexual, and racial others the world-over dialectically respond by seeking equality of opportunity, recognition, and distribution within the class division and social relations of production of the capitalist world-system for themselves and their masses.

Postcolonial, postmodern, and post-structural theories are the academic and political discourse of globalization and postindustrial capitalist relations of production of the contemporary age. The concepts, i.e., ambivalence, double consciousness, créolité, négritude, intersectionality, etc., developing from these theories represent the psychological pathologies and practical consciousness of the bourgeoisies of once discriminated against others within the capitalist world-system. As a result of the emergence of a post-industrial capitalism intent on allowing divergent meanings and individual experiences, which were once discriminated against, to emerge around their class positions for capital accumulation in a service/financial economy focused on entertainment and financial service. Non-class meanings and subjective/individual experiences, homosexuality, transgenderism, black feminism, etc., which were, and to some extent continue to be, discriminated against by both the black underclass and bourgeoisie of earlier capitalist relations of production are fostered and allowed to emerge within the dialectic of the global (postindustrial) capitalist social class structure or relations of production. These non-class meanings and subjective experiences, homosexuality, black feminism, Pan-Africanism, etc., practical consciousnesses, which are the product of the deferment of meaning in ego-centered communicative discourse, contemporarily, are seeking equality of opportunity, recognition, and distribution within the dialectic of a postindustrial capitalist social structure that stratifies and commodifies these non-class identities, meanings, and subjective/individual experiences around their class positions or social relations to production for capital accumulation in the service economies of core, postindustrial nations, such as the US and UK. What has emerged, as a result, are these theories of ambivalence, hybridity, créolité, négritude, double consciousness, and intersectionality among bourgeois academics of once discriminated against others highlighting the discourse by which these variant subjective positions have been alienated, marginalized, and prevented from achieving equality of opportunity, recognition, and distribution within the global (postindustrial) capitalist social structure of racial-class inequality and differentiation. Their theories are universalized and extrapolated globally under the ideological umbrella of identity politics, the fight for social justice, truth, and love. However, by no means can these theories, as applied in the black diaspora be viewed, against the discourse of the pathological-pathogenic and adaptive-vitality positions, as the universal mechanism by which black consciousnesses and communities were constituted. Their rhetoric, like black consciousnesses and black communities in the US, UK, Africa, and the diaspora, are the by-product of the global (industrial and postindustrial) capitalist social structure of class inequality and differentiation and its ideological apparatuses, which attempts to interpellate and structure the practices of subjective experiences within class differentiation and thereby control the practices of diversity and meaning constitution, which contemporarily juxtaposes the bodies, language, ideology, and material conditions of a transnational, multiracial, multicultural, multisexual, etc., upper-class of owners and high-level executives against the bodies, language, ideology, and material conditions of a transnational, multiracial, multicultural, mulitsexual underclass in poverty the world-over seeking equality of opportunity, recognition, and distribution with the former. The postmodern, post-structural, post-colonial theories of ambivalence, hybridity, créolité, négritude, double consciousness, and intersectionality are the concepts, psychological processes, pathologies, and practical consciousness of the bourgeoisies of the once-discriminated against, and do not represent the nature of identity constitution.

Given the neglect of this (historical) relational problem and the Cartesian (transcendental) ontological and epistemological problematic in the writings of post-sixties and post-segregationist era blacks to understanding black practical consciousnesses, contemporarily, the purpose of the present work is to historically understand the origins of double consciousness, intersectionality, and the constitution of black communities and consciousnesses by focusing on black practical consciousnesses, i.e., the ideas the majority of blacks recursively reorganize and reproduce in their material practices to constitute their being-in-the-world or the capitalist social structure of inequality of the United States (US), United Kingdom (UK), Africa, and the diaspora. Within this structurationist logic, we demonstrate our African-Americanization of the black diaspora hypothesis by the two structurally differentiated social class language games of the black American community, a black underclass under the leadership of rappers, athletes, and gangstas and a black bourgeoisie under the leadership of educated professionals and preachers. Both groups are interpellated and embourgeoised by different ideological apparatuses of the capitalist social structure of racial-class inequalities, the church and schools for the latter and the streets, prisons, and poor schools for the former, and blacks who are similarly situated seek to emulate their practical consciousness.

Chapter Two

Phenomenological Structuralism

While we accept the double consciousness and intersectional theories of Gilroy, West, hooks, and Patricia Hill Collins to be the rhetoric of their middle class embourgeoised positions as they stand against the "bling bling" class rhetoric of the black underclasses of the world constituted within and by the Protestant global (postindustrial) capitalist social structure of class inequality/differentiation and its ideological apparatuses. We do not deny the epistemological basis for either their doubleness discourse or postmodern and post-structural theoretical assumptions regarding the indeterminacy of meaning in ego-centered communicative discourse or the notion of the decentered subject to account for social agency in the development of consciousness in general and black consciousness in particular. Our position, however, is that the basis of such rhetoric is two-fold. First it is an under analysis for understanding the origins and basis for the constitution of human consciousness. Second, such rhetoric should be understood within and as being constituted by the dialectical structure of a global capitalist social structure of racial-class inequality and differentiation put in place, through mode of production, language, ideology, ideological state and transnational apparatuses, and communicative discourse, in order to limit, direct, and integrate the meaning and discursive practices of subjective identities, which may arise as a result of the decentered subject and the indeterminacy of meaning in ego-centered communicative discourse. Hence to understand the historical constitution of double consciousness, intersectionality, and the practical consciousness of black communities throughout the world, we must attempt to synthesize the rhetoric of black double consciousness and postmodern and post-structural theorizing, which accurately points out the problematic with attempting to understand the constitution of identities through the notions of the indeterminacy of meaning and the decentered subject, with structural Marxist dialectics, which highlights the class division and capitalist social structure of inequality put in place, through mode of production, language, ideology, ideological state and transnational apparatuses, and communicative discourse, to limit the practices of the indeterminate meanings and subjective positions allowed to organize and reproduce in a structural world organized for capital accumulation and class differentiation. To this end, we use a hermeneutical variant of structuration theory, what Paul C. Mocombe (2013, 2014, 2015) calls phenomenological structuralism, to account for the indeterminacy of meaning, black social agency, and the sociohistorical and ontological development of black practical consciousnesses within and by the American and British dominated global capitalist social structure of racial-class inequality. In other words, we take an ontological approach, as encapsulated in Paul C. Mocombe's (2013, 2014, 2015, 2016) structuration theory, to understanding the constitution of black practical consciousness within the structure of class division, social relations of production, and ideological apparatuses by which the world is organized under American hegemony.

BACKGROUND OF THE PROBLEM

The structurationist or praxis school in the social sciences is commonly associated with Jürgen Habermas (1987 [1981], 1984 [1981]), Pierre Bourdieu (1990 [1980], 1984), and Anthony Giddens (1984) in sociology, and Marshall Sahlins (1976, 1995 [1981]) in anthropology (Crothers, 2003; Ortner, 1984). Elaborated in a series of theoretical works and empirical studies, structurationists or praxis theorists account for agency and consciousness in social structure or system, "by clamping action and structure together in a notion of 'practice' or 'practises'" (Crothers, 2003, pg., 3). That is, structures are not only external to social actors, as in the classic structural functional view, but are also internal rules and resources produced and reproduced by actors "unconsciously" (intuitively) in their practices. That is to say, in structurationist or praxis theory, as Marx one-hundred years before suggested, the structure is "not a substantially separable order of reality", but "simply the 'ideal' form in which the totality of 'material' relations…are manifested to consciousness…" (Sayer, 1987, pg., 84). From this perspective, accordingly, structure or, sociological speaking, social structure, "may set [(ideological)] conditions to the historical process, but it is dissolved and reformulated in material practice [(through mode of production and ideological apparatuses)], so that history becomes the realization, in the form of society, of the actual [(embodied rules)] resources people put into play" (Sahlins, 1995 [1981], pg., 7): consciousness, as a result, refers to "practical consciousness" or the dissolution and reformulation of a social structure's terms (norms, values, prescriptions, and proscriptions) in material practice.

Although this Neo-Marxist "clamping together" of structure, praxis, and consciousness descriptively accounts for "the individual moment of phenomenology" by explaining the unanimity, closure, and "intentionality" of a form of human action or sociation, the capitalist social (material) relations of production and its class division and differentiation, which constitutes the integrative actions of modern society, it fails, however, as pointed out in the epistemological postmodern/post-structural positions of hooks and Collins, to account for the origins and nature of fully visible alternative forms of practices (i.e., "the variability of the individual *moments* of phenomenology") within the dominant order that are not class based, but are the product of the deferment of meaning in ego-centered communicative discourse, i.e., homosexuality, transgenderism, etc. Structurationists, especially Pierre Bourdieu (1984) in essence culturalize the practices emanating from the structural reproduction and differentiation of capitalist class divisions. Be that as it may, they, like the classic structural-functional and structural-Marxist theorizing of the pathological-pathogenic school, fail to see that society and its dominant institutionalized identity is not "one-dimensional" and differentiated by the dialectic of capitalist social relations of production, but is constituted, through power relations, as transition, relation, and difference. This difference, akin to Jacques Derrida's *différance*, is not biologically (racially) hardwired in the social actor, as the adaptive-vitality school suggests, but is a result of self-reflective and non-impulsive social actors, upon internalizing the arbitrary structural terms or signifiers of their society via a transcendental ego of the brain, bodies, language, and linguistic communication, conceiving of and exercising other forms of being-in-the-world from that of the dominant symbolic order and its structural differentiation or relational logic (Habermas, 1987 [1981], 1984 [1981]; Giddens, 1984; Mocombe et al, 2014).

By "clamping" action, structure, and consciousness together, i.e., part/whole totality, however, structurationists do not account for, nor demonstrate, the nature and relation of this non-biologically and non-impulsive determined difference (*différance*) to that of the dominant practices of the social structure as highlighted in the theorizing of postmodern and post-structural scholars. Instead, they re-introduce the problem in a new form: How do we know or *exercise* anything at odds with an embodied received view grounded in, and differentiated by, capitalist social relations of production? Mocombe's phenomenological structural model seeks to fix the duality concept of structurationism to account for this problematic.

To this end of fixing structurationism to account for alternative practical consciousnesses outside the structural reproduction and differentiation of capitalist relations of production, phenomenological structuralism as a metaphysical materialism builds (metaphorically and figuratively) on the material relationship highlighted in physics between the identity and indeterminate behavior of subatomic particles highlighted in quantum mechanics and the determinate behavior of atomic particles in their aggregation as highlighted in general relativity. The purpose of the aforementioned is to understand the material constitution of consciousness at the subatomic/neuronal level in, and as, the brain and its manifestation as human practical consciousness at the atomic level as revealed by a transcendental ego, language, ideology, ideological apparatuses, and the actions of the body.

THEORY

According to the tenets of quantum physics as reflected in supersymmetry theory, dark matter, parallel universes (multiverses), and the EPR paradox, the universe is composed of ordinary matter (atoms and molecules) and dark matter (axions, wimps, neutrinos, bosons, and fermions).[1] Dark matter, as opposed to ordinary matter, constitutes over eighty percent of the material substance that constitute the cosmos. This dark matter is not constituted by atoms and molecules like ordinary matter but consists of subatomic particles and energy. The particles in the nature of quarks are identified as wimps or axions, very tiny particles that contribute to the formation of nuclear components. These tiny particles are conceived of as coiled energies, strings of space-time, packets of energy-like photons. They are physical in nature but immaterial, and coexist, in a parallel/alternate universe, with ordinary matter in the same location without impediment or interference. They belong to the fermion family of invisible particles whose counterparts are named a boson, which is pure energy. So, as highlighted in supersymmetry theory, for every boson particle of matter, a symmetry counterpart, fermion, exists which manifests itself as force or energy. Thus, for every reality we discover in the solid world around us, we must assume that there exists a symmetric counterpart, or boson, which is invisible but is nevertheless as physical as its visible counterpart. These supersymmetric doubles constitute the backbone of alternate realities, parallel universes that are displayed in ten dimensions, including our ordinary three-dimensional Cartesian reality. Moreover, according to the EPR paradox, these particles have psychic properties. That is, the particles are conscious. They are aware of their position, of themselves, and of their surroundings. In other words, the multiverses created by these particles are endowed with consciousness.

Hence the multiverse originated either by fiat or quantum fluctuation. It is a bosonic force that was brought forth together with a fermion counterpart. It is also the primeval pan-psychic field whose fermion can be called a psychion, a particle of consciousness. These have evolved together to produce the four forces of nature, electromagnetic force; gravity; the strong nuclear force; and weak nuclear force, in our universe, which in turn produced atoms, molecules, and aggregated life. In other words, according to quantum mechanics subatomic particles of energy constitute all the matter of the universe via the Higgs Boson Field, i.e., the god particle, which objectifies and materialize the matter that we are, see, hear, taste, feel, and touch. Subatomic particles constitute our material bodies and consciousness as neuronal energies, which constitute and operate the brain and the body. However, subatomic matter, which are strings at the subatomic particle level, operate differently from observable objectified energy, matter, in that their behavior are indeterminate and can exist in, and constitute, multiple places, dimensions or parallel universes, simultaneously prior to being observed or even during observation as aggregated matter. In fact, the subatomic particles that constitute our material bodies and consciousness as neuronal energies are the same subatomic particles that constitute everything that we consider to be the world, universe, other species, etc. At the subatomic particle level we are not subjects contemplating an object, i.e., the world, multiverse, etc., we are the world, an undifferentiating energy. Hence, the implication suggested by the Standard Model of physics is that the observable and non-observable matter that constitutes our universe exists elsewhere in other unseen dimensions and parallel universes simultaneously with our own dispensation of space-time. Contrary to the Copenhagen interpretation of quantum mechanics, we do not occupy a universe. We are part of a multiverse with a plethora of I (s) and other sentient beings existing in them indistinguishable from one another at the subatomic level as energy. They become distinguishable at the atomic level through subatomic particle aggregation, i.e., matter. Subatomic particles aggregate to form objectified matter, universes, worlds, species and sentient beings with consciousness, etc. The plethora of I (s) and other sentient beings are constituted and connected via subatomic particles that are recycled throughout and as the multiverse to constitute and operate consciousness as subatomic neuronal energies of the body and the brain, which encounters objectified matter as objectified matter via the actions and senses of the brain, body, language, ideologies, ideological apparatuses, modes of production, and communicative discourse. In essence, consciousness is recycled subatomic energies of the multiverse objectified and embodied, similar to Hegel's conceptualization of *Geist*. Whereas for Hegel *Geist* is distinct from the material world and unfolds dialectically in it, via embodiment of certain individuals, towards an ever-increasing rationalization of the world towards self-knowledge and freedom. For Mocombe the historical manifestation, Being-in-Spacetime, of the objectification of subatomic particles of the universe as consciousnesses and bodies has no definitive end-goal and is indeterminate. But constrained in materialized space-time by our material bodies and power relations or the social class language games, dualism, of those whose objectification, i.e., historicity, precedes our own individual consciousnesses and control the economic conditions of a material resource framework, which they reify via mode of production, language, ideologies, ideological apparatuses, and communicative discourse.

Like the laws of physics, which attempt to regulate and determine subatomic particle activity as general law (Theory of general relativity) once they are aggregated in our dispensation of space-time, the social class language game of those who control the economic conditions of a material resource framework attempts to regulate and determine the indeterminacy of meaning unfolding in and as the consciousnesses of social actors via bodies, mode of production, language, ideology, ideological apparatuses, and communicative discourse. Unlike, postmodern and post-structural theorizing, which utilize the indeterminacy of meaning as highlighted by the unconscious in the psychoanalytic works of Sigmund Freud and Jacques Lacan, Mocombe's phenomenological structuralism analogously builds on the material relationship in physics between the identity and indeterminate behavior of subatomic particles highlighted in quantum mechanics and the determinate behavior of atomic particles in their aggregation as highlighted in general relativity to understand the material constitution of consciousnesses at the subatomic/neuronal level in, and as, the brain and their manifestation as human practical consciousnesses, via the body, at the atomic level. Mocombe does not, unlike psychoanalysts like Lacan and Freud or phenomenologists like Edmund Husserl, claim to know how the embodiment of recycled subatomic neuronal energies via the microtubules of the brain come to constitute consciousnesses in the brain and their subsequent revelation as the practical consciousnesses of bodies. That is, the transcendental ego or I of a differentiated individual subject, which we do not have access to, could just as much be the past I, recycled subatomic particles, of a sentient being from an alternative universe or dimension of the multiverse and not necessarily the product of repression and the rule of the father, i.e., social construction. Psychoanalysis and the indeterminacy of the processes of the unconscious and the universal mapping of consciousnesses, i.e., its form of understanding, by Edmund Husserl's transcendental phenomenology and contemporary neuroscientists, in other words, neither adequately captures the indeterminate behavior of embodied recycled subatomic particles as neuronal energies of the brain and the myriad of practical consciousnesses they may produce as revealed by diverse practices of bodies, nor can they account for the origins of the transcendental ego or I. Husserl, Freud, and contemporary neuroscientists attempt to highlight and capture the Kantian form of the understanding and sensibilities of the aggregated body and brain, which is unable to explain how aggregated subatomic quantum particles give rise to the transcendental ego of consciousness, which produces praxis. We are not claiming that Mocombe's phenomenological structural ontology captures this process. The only thing of consciousness, produced by embodied subatomic particles, that

Mocombe claims to be ontogenetically universal is the stance of the transcendental ego, what Heidegger calls the *analytic of Dasein*, vis-à-vis the drives of the aggregated body, impulses of recycled past consciousnesses of subatomic particle energies, language, ideology, ideological apparatuses, structural reproduction and differentiation, once it becomes constituted by subatomic particles. Hence the use of phenomenology in phenomenological structuralism. Mocombe holds on to the phenomenological logic of Husserl, Heidegger, Maurice Merleau-Ponty, and Sartre here to capture, in a behavioral sense, the how, via Heidegger's three stances ready-to-hand, unready-to-hand, present-at-hand, of identity constitution amidst indeterminacy of consciousnesses and actions produced by embodied recycled subatomic neuronal energies/particles.

It is the stance of a transcendental ego (embodiment of the primeval pan-psychic field) vis-à-vis 1) the drives of the aggregated body, 2) the drives or impulses of recycled subatomic particles, 3) structural reproduction and differentiation of ideologies, ideological apparatuses, and mode of production, and 4) the deferment of meaning in ego-centered communicative discourse, which determines our practical consciousness. In other words, phenomenological structuralism seeks to highlight the phenomenology of being-in-the-structure-of-those-who-control-a-material-resource-framework and the origins of our practical consciousness. What Mocombe suggests is that embodiment is the objectification of the transcendental ego, which is a part of an universal *élan vital* (Henri Bergson's term), the primeval pan-psychic field, that has ontological status in dimensions existing at the subatomic particle level and gets embodied via, and as, the body and connectum of Being's brains. Hence the transcendental ego is the universal *élan vital*, the primeval pan-psychic field, which is the neuronal energies of past, present, and future Beings-of-the-multiverse, embodied. This transcendental ego, and its stance, encounters a material world via and as the body and brain in mode of production, language, ideology, ideological apparatuses, and communicative discourse.

Once embodied in and as human individual consciousnesses in a particular universe, world, and historical social formation, the transcendental ego becomes an embodied hermeneutic structure that never encounters the world and the things of the world in themselves via the aggregated built-in genetic ontology of the body and the impulses of the neuronal energies, which constituted it. Instead embodied hermeneutic individual consciousness is constituted via the recycled subatomic neuronal particle energies which are aggregated as a transcendental ego and the body in their encounter and interpretation of past recycled neuronal memories and things enframed in and by the language, bodies, ideology, ideological apparatuses, practices, and communicative discourses of those who control the economic conditions of a material resource framework and its social relations of production. In consciousness, as phenomenology posits, it (individual subjective consciousness of embodied beings) can either choose to accept the structural knowledge, differentiation, and practices of the body; the impulses of recycled past consciousnesses of subatomic neuronal particles; the ideologies of those who control, via their bodies, mode of production, language, ideology, ideological apparatuses, and communicative discourse, the economic conditions of the material resource framework and recursively reorganize and reproduce them in their practices; or reject them, given the ability to defer meaning in ego-centered communicative discourse, for an indeterminate amount of action-theoretic ways-of-being-in-the-world-with-others, which they may assume at the threat to their ontological security. It is Being's stance, ready-to-hand, unready-to-hand, and present-at-hand vis-à-vis 1) the drives of the body, 2) impulses of residual actions/memories of embodied recycled past consciousnesses, 3) the phenomenological meditation/deferment that occurs on the latter actions via linguistic communication, and 4) ideologies of a social system along with its differentiating logic, coupled with the will of those in power positions, which produces the variability of actions and practices in cultures, social structures, or social systems that enframe the material world.

As such, as in Heidegger's phenomenology, phenomenology in phenomenological structuralism is not just transcendental, it is also hermeneutical. The act of interpretation (based on the stance of Being) or an embodied hermeneutic structure via the body, language, ideology, and communicative discourse is a universal precondition of being-in-the-world-with-other-human-beings. However, whereas Heidegger is interested in the question of the meaning of Being-as-such, i.e., the phenomenology of Being, phenomenological structuralism is concerned with the *sociology of Being*, the question of the meaning or constitutive nature of embodied Being-as-such's-being-in-the-world-with-others who attempt to constrain practical consciousnesses via their bodies, language, ideologies, ideological apparatuses, and communicative discourse derived from social relations of production. That is, as in Martin Heidegger's phenomenological ontology, Mocombe is interested in the necessary societal relationship and practical consciousnesses that emerge out of the phenomenology of Being-in-the-world-within-structures-of-signification-of-others, who control the economic conditions of the material resource framework we find ourselves existing in, that presuppose our historicity, and Being's perceptions, responses, and practices, i.e., relations, to these structures-of-signification in order to be in the world. Unlike Heidegger, however, the concern is not with the phenomenology of being-in-the-world as such because Being never encounters the world and its transcendental ego as the-thing-itself. Instead being encounters the world via its body/brain, recycled (impulses of) past consciousnesses, and structures of signification, which derive from class division and social relations of production as reified in the bodies (as agential initiative), language, ideology, ideological apparatuses, and communicative discourse of those who control the resources of a material resource framework.

Be that as it may, whereas Mocombe accepts the Husserlian phenomenological understanding that the facts of the world and their conditions of possibility are present in consciousness, i.e., the notion of intentionality, consciousness is always consciousness of something as we experience being-in-the-world-with-other-beings via our consciousness, i.e., transcendental ego, bodies, language, ideologies, and communicative discourse. Mocombe's position, however, is that as an embodied hermeneutic structured being we never experience the facts of the world and their conditions of possibility as the "the things in themselves." We experience them not culturally and historically, which is a present-at-hand viewpoint, but structurally and relationally, via the bodies, language, ideology, and communicative discourse in institutions or ideological apparatuses, i.e., the social class language game, of those who control the economic conditions of the material resource framework we find ourselves thrown-in, via our bodies, language, and communicative discourse. In other words, Mocombe's phenomenology of embodied Being-in-the-world-as-such's-Being-with-others, phenomenological structuralism, synthesizes Merleau-Ponty's and Heidegger's phenomenology with Karl Marx's materialism and Ludwig Wittgenstein's language game to suggest that being-in-the-world with others, our practical consciousness, is a product of our interpretation, acceptance, or rejection of the symbols of signification, social class language game, of those bodies in institutional/ideological power positions who control via their bodies, language, ideologies, ideological apparatuses, and communicative discourse the economic conditions of a material resource framework as we encounter them and their symbols/signifiers in institutions or ideological apparatuses via our own transcendental ego, bodies, language, and communicative discourse. Hence we never experience the things-in-themselves of the world culturally and historically in consciousness. We experience them structurally or relationally, and our stances, ready-to-hand, unready-to-hand, present-at-hand, vis-à-vis these ideological structures determine our practical consciousness or behaviors.

We initially know, experience, and utilize the things of the world in the preontological ready-to-hand mode, which is structural and relational. That is, our bodies and impulses encounter, know, experience, and utilize the things of the world in consciousness, intersubjectively, via their representation as objects of knowledge, truth, usage, and experience enframed and defined in the relational logic and practices or language game (Wittgenstein's term) of the institutions or ideological apparatuses of the other beings-of-the-material resource framework whose historicity comes before our own and gets reified in and as language, ideology, ideological apparatuses, and communicative discourse based on their mode of production or satisfying the needs of the aggregated body. This is the predefined phenomenal structural, i.e., ontological, world we, the psychion or transcendental ego of the primeval pan-psychic field, and our bodies are thrown-in in coming to be-in-the-world. How an embodied-hermeneutically-structured Being as such solipsistically goes on to view, experience, understand, and utilize the predefined objects of knowledge, truth, and experienced defined by others and their conditions of possibilities in consciousness in order to formulate their practical consciousness is albeit indeterminate. Heidegger is accurate, however, in suggesting that three stances or modes of encounter (Analytic of Dasein), "presence-at-hand," "readiness-to-hand," and "un-readiness-to-hand," characterizes our views of the things of consciousness represented intersubjectively via bodies, language, ideology, and communicative discourse, and subsequently determine our practical consciousness or social agency. In "ready-to-hand," which is the preontological mode of human existence thrown in the world, we accept and use the things in consciousness with no conscious experience of them, i.e., without thinking about them or giving them any meaning or signification outside of their intended usage. Heidegger's example is that of using a hammer in hammering. We use a hammer without thinking about it or giving it any other condition of possibility outside of its intended usage as defined by those whose historicity presupposes our own. In "present-at-hand," which, according to Heidegger, is the stance of science, we objectify the things of consciousness and attempt to determine and reify their meanings, usage, and conditions of possibilities. Hence the hammer is intended for hammering by those who created it as a thing solely meant as such. The "unready-to-hand" outlook is assumed when something goes wrong in our usage of a thing of consciousness as defined and determined by those who adopt a "present-at-hand" view. As in the case of the hammer, the unready-to-hand view is assumed when the hammer breaks and we have to objectify it, by then assuming a present-at-hand position, and think about it in order to either reconstitute it as a hammer, or give it another condition of possibility. Any other condition of possibility that we give the hammer outside of its initial condition of possibility which presupposed our historicity becomes relational, defined in relation to any of its other conditions of possibilities it may have been given by others we exist in the world with. Hence for Heidegger, the ontological status of being-in-the-world-with-others, via these three stances or modes of encountering the objects of consciousness hermeneutically reveal, through our view, experience, understanding, and usage of the predefined objects of knowledge, truth, and experience. Whereas Heidegger in his phenomenological work goes on to deal with the existential themes of anxiety, alienation, death, despair, etc., in Mocombe's phenomenological stance regarding societal constitution or Beings-as-such's-being-in-the-world-with-others via our stances to the body, language, ideology, ideological apparatuses, communicative discourse, and social relations of production he is not concerned with the phenomenological preoccupation of individual solipsistic existence as defined in Jean-Paul Sartre's work which claims to take off from Heidegger. Instead, he is interested in the universal ontological structure, i.e., social structure or societal constitution and practical consciousness, which arises out of Heidegger's three stances vis-à-vis embodiment, language, ideology, ideological apparatuses, communicative discourse, and social relations of production. That is, Mocombe is not concerned with Sartre's phenomenologization of the Cartesian *res cogitans*/ transcendental ego, i.e., the present-at-hand transcendental ego, which he gives ontological status in the world as a solipsistic individual seeking to define themselves for themselves lest they be declared living in bad faith. The overemphasis of that particular aspect of *Dasein*, according to Mocombe, is a product of a specific historical and relational mode of production, and only account for one of its analytics as highlighted by Heidegger. For Mocombe, the transcendental ego, which is a part of a universal *élan vital*, the primeval pan-psychic field, existing in another dimension at the subatomic particle level, does not originate out of the historical material world, but several variations of it becomes objectified via embodiment and the aforementioned stances in a universe, galaxy, and historical material world structured by other embodied Beings and their stances. Upon death its historicity via subatomic neuronal particles gets reabsorbed into the *élan vital*, primeval pan-psychic field, to be recycled to produce future beings. As such consciousness, i.e., practical consciousness, is a product of the stances of *Dasein* vis-à-vis its embodied recycled past consciousnesses/impulses, language and ideology, which can be deferred in ego-centered communicative discourse, and structural reproduction and differentiation determined by mode of production, ideological apparatuses, and those in power positions. Be that as it may, as with Heidegger, who refutes Sartre's existential rendering of his phenomenological ontology, Mocombe is interested in the objectified/reified societal constitution and practical consciousnesses of the transcendental egos and their relations that emerge within a dominant constitution of Being that controls a material resource framework of the world via bodies, mode of production, language, ideology, ideological apparatuses, and communicative discourse vis-à-vis the stances of the transcendental ego.

Consciousnesses for us, building on Mocombe's phenomenological structuralism, then are the embodiment of recycled subatomic neuronal energies of the multiverse objectified in the space-time of multiple universes as aggregated matter. Once objectified and embodied the neuronal energies encounter the space-time of physical worlds via a transcendental subject of consciousnesses, languages, and the senses of the body and brain in structures of signification, language, ideology, and ideological apparatuses, defined and determined by other beings that control the resources of the material world required for physical survival in space-time. The actions produced via either the present-at-hand, ready-to-hand, or unready-to-hand gaze of consciousness vis-à-vis 1) the drives/impulses of subatomic particles, 2) the drives/impulses of the aggregated body and brain, 3) the ability to defer meaning of signifiers as they appear to consciousnesses in ego-centered communicative discourse, and 4) the differentiating effects of the structures of signification, social class language game, of those who control the materials of a world is the origins of practical consciousnesses. As such, phenomenological structuralism synthesizes, the notions of the materialism and indeterminacy of behavior of subatomic particles in quantum mechanics as they get objectified as neuronal energies of the brain to produce the transcendental subject of consciousness; with the multiplicity of and for meaning in Heideggerian phenomenology to capture the process of indeterminacy and deferment of meaning highlighted by postmodern and post-structural theory; with Marxist dialectic and Wittgensteinian notions of language games to highlight the atomic structures, mode of production, bodies, language, ideology, and ideological apparatuses, collectively understood here under the concept social class language game, which attempt to structure the indeterminacy of consciousness at the atomic human level as revealed in the practices, i.e., practical consciousnesses, of social actors.

The notion of *social class language game* utilized here is an adoption of the "language-games" later philosophy of Ludwig Wittgenstein (1951) conceptualized within a Marxian understanding of the constitution of identities based on the practical consciousness and ideology of those who control the economic conditions, social relations of production, of a material resource framework. For the Wittgenstein of the *Philosophical Investigations* language is a tool and must be thought of as a rule-governed, self-contained practice, like a game, of activities associated with some particular family of linguistic expressions, which have no point outside themselves, but is simply associated with the satisfactions they give to the participants and their form of life. What we are suggesting here, against the genetic ontology of Christopher Macann (1993) who views the transcendental ego as "a subjectification of embodied human being," in our phenomenological ontology, phenomenological structuralism, which seeks to highlight the phenomenology of being-in-the-structure-of-those-who-control-a-material-resource-framework
through language, bodies, ideology, ideological apparatuses, and the social relations of production, is that embodiment is the objectification of the transcendental ego, which is a part of an universal *élan vital* (which is a material thing, the subatomic particles of past consciousnesses, the eternal recurrence of past consciousnesses, that gets encapsulated in and as the brain of breathing subjects we see in any given historical formation) that has ontological status in dimensions existing at the subatomic particle level and gets embodied via, and as, the connectome of Beings' brains and their bodies. Embodiment is the multiverse manifesting itself as embodied consciousness or a transcendental ego. Once objectified, materialized, and embodied as

human individual consciousnesses in a present historical formation or social structure the transcendental ego becomes an embodied hermeneutic structure that never encounters the world and the things of the world in themselves as highlighted by Jacques Lacan through his conception of the symbolic; instead embodied hermeneutic individual consciousnesses are constituted via recycled past consciousnesses, the body, language, and ego-centered communicative discourse in their encounter and interpretation of things enframed in and by the historical consciousness, language, bodies, ideology, ideological apparatuses, and practices of those who control the economic conditions, social relations of production, of the material resource framework it finds itself thrown in. As embodied consciousness, whose ideas and practices are revealed and manifested through the body and language, it (individual consciousnesses of beings) can either accept the signified historical structural knowledge, differentiation, and practices (social class language game as revealed by the language, ideology, and ideological apparatuses) of those who control the economic conditions, social relations of production, of the material resource framework and recursively reorganize and reproduce them in their practices and institutions, or reject them, given the ability to defer meaning in ego-centered communicative discourse, for an indeterminate amount of action-theoretic ways-of-being-in-the-world-with-others, which they may assume at the threat to their ontological security. It is the manifestation of actions deriving from the gaze of the being vis-à-vis 1) the impulses/drives of recycled subatomic particles, 2) the form of sensibilities of the body and brain, 3) the phenomenological meditation and deferment of meaning that occurs in embodied consciousness via language, ideology, and communicative discourse as reflected in diverse individual practices, 4) within the differentiating logic or class divisions of the social relations of production, which produces the variability of actions and practices in cultures, social structures, or social systems. All four types of actions, drives/impulses of recycled subatomic particles, the drive of the body/brain, structural reproduction/differentiation, and actions resulting from the deferment of meaning in ego-centered communicative discourse, are always present and manifested in a social structure (which is the reified ideology via ideological apparatuses of those who control a material resource framework) to some degree contingent upon the will and desires of the economic social class that controls the material resource framework through its language, symbols, ideology, ideological apparatuses, and social relations of production. They choose, amidst the class division of the social relations of production, what other meaning constitutions and practices are allowed to manifest themselves without facing alienation, marginalization, domination, or death.

In sum, phenomenological structuralism posits consciousness (practical consciousness) to be the by-product or evolution of subatomic particles unfolding with increasing levels of abstraction. Subatomic particles, via the

Higgs boson particle, gave rise to carbon atoms, molecules and chemistry, which gave rise to DNA, biological organisms, neurons and nervous systems, which aggregated into brains that gave rise to consciousnesses and languages. In human beings, the indeterminate behavior of subatomic neuronal energies in the brain that produced the plethora of consciousnesses and languages gave rise to ideologies, which in turn gave rise to ideological apparatuses and societies (sociology) under the social class language game or bodies, consciousness, language, ideology, and ideological apparatuses of those who control the material resources required for physical survival in a particular resource framework. So contrary to Karl Marx's materialism which posits human consciousness to be the product of material conditions, the logic here is that the aggregated human being is a linguistic abstraction that never encounters the material world directly. Instead, they encounter the world via structures of signification, which structures the world or a particular part of it through the body, historical consciousness, language, ideology, and ideological apparatuses, i.e., social class language game, of those whose power and power positions dictate how the resources of that framework are to be gathered, used, and distributed (means and mode of production). Hence unlike Marx, which views the origins of modern capitalist relations of production via the notion of primitive accumulation, phenomenological structural ontology is in agreement with Max Weber and views it as the product of the structures of signification of Protestant Christianity, i.e., the Protestant Ethic and the spirit of capitalism.

PHENOMENOLOGICAL STRUCTURALISM DIAGRAMMATICALLY

Hence phenomenological structuralism agrees with the structurationists that in the constitution of society the individual elements incorporate the structure of the whole and get differentiated by the relational logic of that whole. Our understanding, unlike that of the traditional structurationists, attempts to provide an analytical tool to explain and examine the relation of the "others" within the totality who do not, however: the relationship between "the individual elements [, who,] internalize [and recursively reproduce,] the structur[ing ideology] of the whole," and those who as a result of their ready-to-hand, unready-to-hand, and present-at-hand stances vis-à-vis the drives of their bodies, impulses of residual past consciousnesses of recycled subatomic particles or through self- reflection or phenomenological meditation in the unready-to-hand and present-at-hand mode of encountering the structural terms of a society conceive of, or choose among, fully visible "alternative" ways of being-in-the-world, which they attempt to exercise in the "totality."

This "mechanical" relationship can be expressed diagrammatically (see Figure 2.1), and is an adaptation of Stephen Slemon's (1995) description of colonialism's multiple strategies for regulating Europe's others (Slemon, 1995, pg. 46), and the way we see it, whether in our usage of it or Slemon's slightly different depiction, it is a macro, at the societal level, extrapolation of Hegel's and Marx's master/slave dialectical power model, which would proceed along line A1, since we both suppose that our respective concepts (colonialism for Selmon and society, culture, structure, what have you, for us) are ideological or discursive formations constituted through power relations.[2]

The general understanding, within a phenomenological structural understanding of the constitution of society and practical consciousness, is that individual actors or network of solidarity or cultural groups (irreducibly "mediating" situated subjects), represented by lines "A" and "B" on the diagram, are relationally socialized within society—its semiotic field or predefined and predetermined lexicons and representations of signification (at the bottom of the diagram) i.e., the field of socialization "and its investment in reproducing and naturalising the structures of power" (Slemon, 1995, pg. 47)—through "ideological apparatuses" (at the top of the diagram) controlled by socialized institutional regulators ("As"), power elites or those in power positions, who recursively reorganize and reproduce the rules of conduct (which appear to be natural and commonsensical) of the social structure, which in modern times represent an ideological flanking for the protestant/ capitalist economic subjugation running along line "A1." Where in the first instance (A) there is encountering of the rules of conduct of the society at the preontological ready-to-hand mode of encountering, there is adoption or internalization (the Structurationist view) on behalf of the individual or network of groups of the prescribed understanding of the representations and practices of the semiotic field, i.e., the recursively organized and reproduced rules of conduct which are sanctioned. In the second (B), the individual encounters the facts and values of the world in either unready-to-hand or the present-at-hand mode, and through a form of phenomenological meditation on the structural terms (i.e., norms, values, prescriptions and proscriptions of power) that presuppose their existence, conceives of, or chooses among other or fully visible alternatives (other "Bs" discriminated by the social structure), a different understanding (, i.e., practical means, arriving from the drives of the body, unconscious drives of recycled subatomic particles, or through the deferment of meaning in ego-centered communicative discourse) of being-in-the-world ; or as in the case of racism, sexism, and classism is prescribed a structurally differentiated unalterable subordinate role based on the relational binary logic (rules for inclusion and exclusion) of the semiotic field of those in power positions ("As"). In this structurally differentiated mode the encountering is always either at the ready-to-hand or unready-to-hand mode of encountering, in the latter because something, discriminatory effects of the totality, is wrong in allowing the social actor to partake in the rules of conduct of the society. So regardless if they accept or reject the rules of conduct, they are still classified by the power elites as (Bs)

The socialized individuals or groups ("As")—socialized in the "constitutive power of societal apparatuses like education, and the constitutive power of fields of knowledge [, which stems from the semiotic field,] within those apparatuses" (46)—possess the potential to become, if they so choose, power elites and as such institutional regulators (at the top of the diagram), who subordinate through the manufacture of consent. Now to maintain power, those who become regulators (some "As") must address "B's" signification, which relationally undermines (it gives social actors an "alternative" form of being-in-the-world), as well as define, delimits, and stabilizes the predefined lexicons and representations of signification that is the society's semiotic field. In other words, their ("Bs'") interpretations or structurally differentiated identity in relation to "A's" reject the singularity and realism or naturalism attached to the representations and meanings of the social field, while at the same time helping to constitute it by defining, delimiting, and stabilizing the field, i.e., "B's" interpretation in relation to "A's" helps to define, because it is not, "A's" interpretation. Hence, the "As" must negotiate, appropriate, and reinflect "Bs" interpretive-practices into the semiotic field in order to delimit, their own; this is done, or has been done, up to this point in the human archaeological records on the constitution of society, by having them ("Bs") remain outside the field, by dismissing their interpretive-claims, in which case the field justifies their permanent outsider status (oppressed or discriminated against minorities, i.e., marginalized "other").

The "Bs," for the most part, can either accept (if their gaze is upon the eye of power—"As"—for recognition as a structurally differentiated "other," i.e., a class-in-itself) their appropriation, the rationale the institutional regulators ("As") prescribe to their ("B_1s'''") interpretive-practical consciousness which legitimates it as a representation, or they ("B_2s'''") may choose (by averting their gaze as a class-for-itself) to remain *quasi*-outsiders if the meaning disclosed by the dominant institutional regulators is not in accordance with their own, or a previously discriminated subculture's, interpretive-practical understanding of the signifiers of the social structure. Regardless of what choice they ("Bs") make, however, they, "Bs," because the validity claims the institutional regulators provide for their (Bs') understanding validates their existence to start with, constantly attempt incorporation and acceptance, either, as a "class-in-itself," pushing for integration as a structurally differentiated "other" (hybrid) who recursively reproduce the rules of conduct of the social structure ("B_1s'''"); or separation ("B_2s'''"), as a "class-for-itself," for their own rules of conduct which are sanctioned by the power elites of the subculture. The former is the position of the bourgeoisie's of once discriminated against groups, such as blacks, women, etc., in contemporary postindustrial Protestant capitalist societies seeking to partake as an hybrid other in the social class language games of the society.

Thus there are two fundamental paths which are open to "Bs": first, if they (B) accept the understanding of (A), regarding their interpretation as an "other," and seek integration, as a structurally differentiated "class-in-itself," they have to give up their interpretive-practical consciousness, which on the one hand undermines the legitimation of the interpretive community they are classed with, while on the other hand, legitimating society's semiotic field, which has appropriated their ("Bs'") understanding and representation to substantiate and delimit their (As') power position and "practical consciousness." From this perspective, the "Bs," "B_1s'",who accept appropriation, are socialized (institutionalized) and attempt to live as ("As"), which entail recursively organizing and reproducing, as a hybrid "other," the rules of conduct of the society which are sanctioned. Those who do not (the second path), that is, those in the present-at-hand mode of encountering who reject the rules of conduct of the society, for their own, "B_2s'", may seek to reconstitute society in line with their interpretive-practical consciousness, which gives rise to another (warring) structure of signification or form of being-in-the-world, which, as a segregated categorical boundary or alternative practical consciousness, relationally and differentially delimits that of the society or social structure, which they initially constituted.[3]

From the perspective of power, "As," "Bs'" interpretations, their interpretive-practical consciousness, are always represented in the semiotic field in order to define, delimit, and stabilize the power structure. Thus, "Bs" are always oppressed minorities or majorities, i.e., "others," in the Hegelian master/slave relationship (A1), who must construct their identities or consciousness within two or more ideals: that of the social structure (master's own understanding of themselves) and what it says of the discriminated against "other" (the slave). Hence, the "Bs," as long as their gaze is turned back upon the eyes of power (vector of motion of "B_1s'") for recognition in the unready-to-hand mode of encountering, which seeks to fix the status quo for their participation, pose no real danger to the semiotic field, unless—following the aforementioned second path,"B_2s',"—they should take-up arms against it as a distinct structuring structure, i.e., "class-for-itself" or categorical boundary, which has averted their gaze, and are attempting to preserve or universalize their "alternative" ontology or "practical consciousness." This latter position is represented by Islamic fundamentalists contemporarily, and the African participants of Bois Caiman during the Haitian Revolution.

In other words, in having to construct their (Bs) identities or consciousness by warring against the ideals of the social structure, which become the relational terms that defines, delimits, and stabilizes the social structure and that by which all ("As" and "Bs") must construct their consciousness, the gaze back upon the eye of power is a sign of recognition of the validity claims of the social structure, which necessarily implies that in order to be recognized the "Bs" must attempt to be what they are not, like "As." This agential move to be like "As," however, constrains the variability of practices, which, as the diagram highlights, can only be maintained if the gaze of Bs' (vector of motion of "B_2s'") are averted away from the eyes of power in order to establish another segregated structuring structure, which celebrates and reproduces the practices' of their "otherness." So long as the aim of "B" is for acceptance into the structure of social relations that constitute the society, their "otherness" can only be expressed as those ("As") who recursively reorganize and reproduce the rules of conduct of the social structure. For it is only upon the world of existing state of affairs, i.e., the valid norms and subjective experiences of power, which is taken to be the nature of reality and existence as such, will they ("Bs") be admitted into the structure of social relations that constitute the society, for any other form may undermine the whole of social relations that is the constituted society.[4]

THE ROLE OF POWER IN THE DIAGRAM

Whereas, figure 2.1 demonstrates the action of individual social actors or groups within "a" reified consciousness, social class language game, that forms the structure of relations that is their society, figure 2.2 makes evident the actions of social actors (As), if and when, they become institutional/ideological regulators or power elites.

The understanding here is that it is the legal regulations of a society, its "lexicons and representations of signification," its rules of conduct that are sanctioned, as outlined by the power elites, or institutional regulators in power positions, which represent the objective conditions (social structure) of society that structure social relations and constitute the materials by-which consciousness is to be cultivated for the ontological security of the individual. In other words, the general understanding, within a phenomenological structural understanding, is that individual actors or groups (irreducibly situated subjects), lines A and B, are socialized within society—its semiotic field or predefined and predetermined lexicons and representations of signification (at the bottom of the diagram) i.e., the field of socialization "and its investment in reproducing and naturalising the structures of power" (Slemon, 1995, pg. 47)—through "ideological apparatuses" (at the top of the diagram) controlled by socialized institutional regulators ("As"), which represent an ideological flanking for the economic subjugation running along line "A1." The relation between the two runs this way: societal power operates through a complex relationship between apparatuses (i.e., the law, education, rituals,

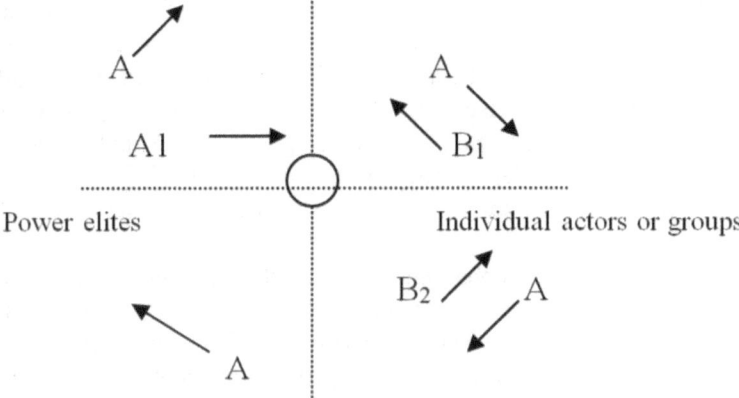

Figure 2.1. Institutional regulators (Society's educational/ideological apparatuses). Diagram representing the nature of the relationship between society and the individual or group in phenomenological structuralism. "A" represent the power elites of the social structure; B_1 represent those "others" (hybrids) with their gaze upon the eye of power seeking to be like "A"; B_2 represent those with their gaze averted from the eye of power seeking to exercise an alternative practical consciousness from that of "As" and "B_1s."

family etc.) placed on line "C," where in the first instance institutional regulators ("As")—at the top of the line—appropriate and manufacture, based on what is already understood, lexicons and representations of signification of individuals in order to consolidate and legitimate itself as a natural "order" and to reproduce individuals as deployable units of that order. So, in the first instance, societal power runs not just through the middle ground of this diagram (A1) but through a complex set of relations happening along line "C;" and since the argument here is that a function (i.e., socialized social actor) at the top of this line is employing those representations created at the bottom of the line in order to make up "knowledges" that have an ideological function, one can say that the vector of motion along line C is an upward one, and that this upward motion is part of the whole complex discursive structure whereby society manufactures individuals and thus helps to regulate societal relations. This is the first position.

The second position, as the diagram demonstrates, is the downward movement of societal power, where the institutional regulators of society's apparatuses are understood to be at work in the production of a purely unique and entirely projected idea of the individual, relationally delimited by other fully visible marginalized "alternative" forms of the individual being-in-the-world. The point this movement, which is inextricably tied to the first, is trying to articulate is that society is a product of the working and reworking of reified psychic projections. Hence, society has to be understood as a structure or system of power relations in which those in power positions attempt to structure, via bodies, language, ideology, ideological apparatuses, and communicative discourse individuals toward an unchangeable unified end.[5] This does not mean that there is no agency, for whom or what acts oppositionally, in this understanding of the constitution of society, is demonstrated through an understanding of the movements of lines A and B described above.

Essentially, then, in this phenomenological structural understanding, society develops from the interpretive-practical consciousness of those (power elites or social actors in power positions) who maintain control of and integrate its material resource framework.[6] Through this economic and political process, all individual actors ("As" and "Bs"), unless they choose (as a "class-for-itself" under the auspices of their own power elites) to establish their own institutions, are socialized in apparatuses controlled by these social actors, institutional regulators (at the top of the diagram), who employ their representations, the reified symbolic objects that constitute the semiotic field (society)—at the bottom of the diagram, in institutions—so as to control, guide, and incorporate the ambivalence that lies in the act of interpretation (Bhabha, 1995, pg. 208)—in order to make up and reproduce ideological "knowledges" that maintain the functioning of the society as a whole.[7] We argue that this Mocombeian model, up to this point in the human archaeological research on societal relations, is a general structure for understanding the multivalent strategies at work in the reproduction and transformation of societies. Furthermore, it resolves the issue of agency, which is problematic when one posits ideology or discourse or psychic processes as constructing human subjects, for who or what acts is clearly demonstrated in the model through the praxis of the structure ("As") and anti-structural elements ("Bs" if they form interpretative communities, "B_2s'", which do not seek incorporation or cooptation).

DISCUSSION AND CONCLUSIONS

The understanding here is that the transcendental ego of Being becomes embodied and objectified in a material resource framework enframed by bodies, the mode of production, language, ideology, ideological apparatuses, and communicative discourse of those who control a material resource framework. As embodied consciousness the transcendental ego initially encounters itself and the world in the ready-to-hand preontological mode. This means as aggregated recycled subatomic particle, aggregated matter, Being is, initially, unconsciously driven by the drives of its body/brain and the

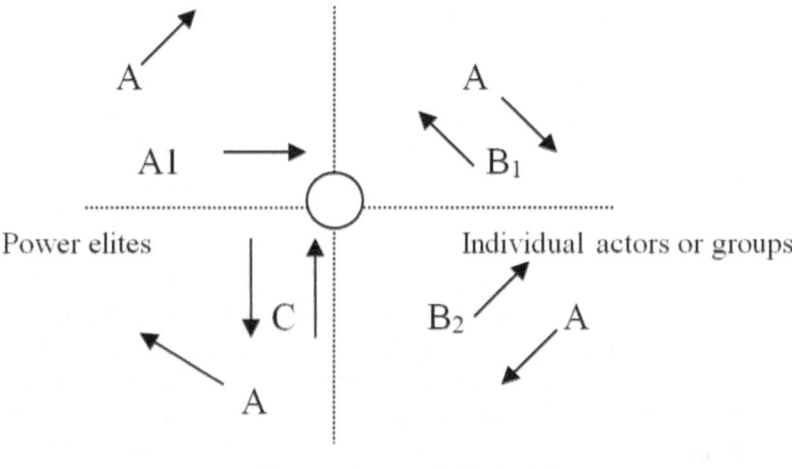

Figure 2.2. Institutional regulators (Society's educational/ideological apparatuses). Diagram representing the nature of the relationship—C—between society's semiotic field (bottom of diagram) and the institutional regulators (top of diagram) in phenomenological structuralism.

agential initiatives of recycled past subatomic neuronal particles as limited by their embodiment. If its bodily and neuronal drives are uninhibited by the bodies, mode of production, language, ideology, ideological apparatuses, and communicative discourse, i.e., social class language game, of those who control the material resource framework, Being may spend all of their existence in this stance. However, should they encounter resistance vis-à-vis their drives and the social class language game of those who control the material resource framework, Being moves to the unready-to-hand stance where they think about and question their own drives/impulses and or those (enframing ideology) of the material resource framework. At which point, they may become present-at-hand and may opt for either the practices associated with their internal drive/impulses, which they reify as culture, or that of the social class language game in power. If they choose the latter, being simply seeks the structural practices and differentiation of power at the expense of their internal drives/impulses. In the former case, choosing to reproduce their internal drives, Being, attempts to recursively reproduce either the drives of its body or what was/is the unconscious drives of recycled past consciousnesses in the conscious present-at-hand stance at the threat to their ontological security in the material resource framework. At which point they may seek other Beings who share their drives or seek to change the ideology of power to accept what has become a decentered subject who has deferred the meaning of power. The latter position is the basis for postmodern and poststructural thought, and alternative practices outside of structural reproduction and differentiation.

From this understanding of consciousness constitution as the product of the drives of subatomic particles, the body, and the indeterminacy of meaning unfolding within structures of signification structured and determined by the dialectic of class division and the social relations of production of those who control, through mode of production and their social class language games, i.e., language, ideology, ideological apparatuses, a material resource framework, we conclude that the majority of black American, British, and diasporic practical life and communities were not initially constituted by their créolité, négritude, hybridity, ambivalence, intersectionality or doubleness, which are the unready-to-hand contemporary bourgeois perspectives of members of a black bourgeois class operating in a postindustrial capitalist social structure of inequality interested in the commodification of subjective experiences for capital accumulation. Instead the indeterminacy of black American, British, and diasporic practical life, community, and consciousness as constituted in the brain and revealed as black practical consciousnesses via their bodies and languages were initially (forcefully) constituted within and by the structure and processes of the dialectic of a Protestant global mercantile, agricultural, and industrial capitalist social structure of racial-class inequality and differentiation, which dates back to the seventeenth century. Black American, British, and diasporic life and communities were initially constituted (interpellated and embourgeoised) and differentiated, ready-to-hand, along racial-class lines, as a racial-caste-in-class, differentiated by the mode of production or organization of labor between a black bourgeoisie and a black underclass, and became dual and pathological in relation to these two particular interpretive communities, the social class language games of the upper-class of white and black owners and high-level corporate executives, i.e., the bourgeoisie, of the two societies as their bodies, language, and material conditions stood in relation to the bodies, language, and material conditions of the poor black underclasses. As such, the majority of the divergences of black life where they existed during the mercantile, agricultural, and industrial capitalism of seventeenth, eighteenth, nineteenth, and early twentieth centuries, were for the most part racial-class-based practices developed relationally in segregated racial-caste-class communities in the United States (US), United Kingdom (UK), and the diaspora that marginalized and discriminated against practices, homosexuality, transgender, etc., that were arrived-at, present-at-hand, either through the drives of recycled subatomic particles, the sensibilities of the body, or the deferment of meaning in ego-centered communicative discourse. The double consciousness discourse of W.E.B. Du Bois, Paul Gilroy, and Cornel West was, and is, the unready-to-hand rhetoric of the black bourgeoisie seeking equality of opportunity, recognition, and distribution for themselves and the black underclasses within the class differentiation of agricultural, industrial, and postindustrial capitalism that prevented and prevents them from doing so even though their practical consciousnesses patterned their white counterparts. Contemporarily, as previously mentioned, as a result of the emergence of a postindustrial capitalism intent on decentering the bourgeois subject and allowing divergent meanings and subjective experiences to emerge around their class positions for capital accumulation in a service economy focused on entertainment and service, non-class meanings and subjective experiences, homosexuality, black feminism, etc., which were, and to some extent continue to be, discriminated against by both the black underclass and bourgeoisie of earlier capitalist relations of production (under slavery and colonialism) are fostered and allowed to emerge within the dialectic of the global (postindustrial) capitalist social class structure. These non-class meanings and subjective experiences, homosexuality, black feminism, Pan-Africanism, etc., practical consciousnesses, which are the product of the deferment of meaning in ego-centered communicative discourse, contemporarily, are, un-ready-to-hand, seeking equality of opportunity, recognition, and distribution within the dialectic of a postindustrial capitalist social structure that stratifies and commodifies these non-class identities, meanings, and subjective experiences around their class positions or social relations to production for capital accumulation in the service economies of core, postindustrial nations, such as the US and UK. What has emerged, as a result, are these unready-to-hand and present-at-hand theories of intersectionality, hybridity, etc., among bourgeois academics highlighting the discourse by which these variant subjective positions have been marginalized and prevented from achieving equality of opportunity, recognition, and distribution within the global (postindustrial) capitalist social structure of class inequality and differentiation of the US and UK. Be that as it may, by no means can double consciousness, hybridity, intersectionality, etc. be viewed, against the discourse of the pathological-pathogenic, adaptive-vitality, anti-essentialist, and anti-anti-essentialist positions, as the universal mechanism by which black consciousnesses and communities were constituted as their rhetoric, like black consciousnesses and black communities in the US, UK, and the diaspora are the unready-to-hand/ present-at-hand by-product of the global (industrial and postindustrial) capitalist social structure of class inequality and differentiation, which attempts to structure, present-at-hand, the practices of subjective experiences within reified class differentiation and thereby control diversity and meaning constitution around class.

Against the contemporary bourgeois notions of hybridity, double consciousness, intersectionality, etc., this work explores and historically unfold, through Mocombe's phenomenological structuralism, how black communities and consciousnesses in the US, UK, and the diaspora were initially constituted, ready-to-hand, as a racial-caste-in-class within and by the dialectic of a global capitalist social structure of class inequality and differentiation that attempted, and attempts, to structure and limit meaning and subjective experiences and practices within the class division and differentiation of capitalism and its processes of capital accumulation. Racial discrimination led to the unready-to-hand discourse of hybridity, double consciousness, ambivalence, intersectionality, etc., among the black bourgeoisie, which sought to recursively reproduce and reorganize the practical consciousness of power as a discriminated against other. Today, they reify their aim in the academy as a present-at-hand viewpoint. We further hypothesize, given American hegemony and the material wealth of the black American underclass and bourgeoisie they have become the bearers of ideological and linguistic domination in the diaspora. Hence, the African Americanization of the black diaspora we go on to demonstrate is an unready-to-hand/present-at-hand epiphenomenon of the black experience vis-à-vis this class division and social relations of production of capitalism under American hegemony and their influence as the bearers of ideological and linguistic domination for black youth and the administrative bourgeoisies of the diaspora in the age of globalization.

NOTES

1. Mocombe's phenomenological structuralism, as in Western epistemology and ontology which developed as a result of the ever-increasing rationalization and testing of Christian notions, reflects his rationalization of Vodou metaphysics as an ontology and sociology for understanding cosmic and societal constitution. As such, Mocombe's work builds off of Reginald O. Crosley's (2006) essay, "Shadow-Matter Universes in Haitian and Dagara Ontologies: A Comparative Study," whose physics we summarize here.

2. For an in-depth look at Slemon's diagram and description see: Slemon, Stephen (994). "The Scramble for Post-colonialism." In *De-Scribing Empire: Post-colonialism and Textuality*, Eds. Chris Tiffin and Alan Lawson. London: Routledge. Slemon borrows this model (see figure 2.1 in the text) from Ferdinand De Saussure (1983 [1916], pg., 80), who prescribes the model as means for all sciences to map out the things they are concerned with. He calls the horizontal axis, "the axis of simultaneity." "This axis concerns relations between things which coexist, relations from which the passage of time is entirely excluded." The vertical axis, "the axis of succession:" "Along this axis one may consider only one thing at a time. But here we find all the things situated along the first axis, together with the changes they undergo."

Slemon, in using this model to understand Edward Said's depiction of colonialism and the role of the "other" argues, as many critics of structuralism have done, that there is no agency regardless of the practices taking place along the diachronic axis (i.e., the vertical axis; the horizontal axis for Saussure is the synchronic). Using this model to depict what Mocombe means by phenomenological structuralism, we argue that Mocombe's description is not historically specific, and resolves the issue of agency in structure (in this case ideological structure or hegemony).

3. Some may point to a third alternative, i.e., subversion from within, but this is a misconception because in order to be a subverter, the social actor must still recursively organize and reproduce the practical consciousness of the whole.

4. In other words, although "Bs" in the diagram represent the variability of praxis within structure, "counter-movements" in the Polanyian (2001 [1944]) sense only refer to embodied

variable practices—which diametrically oppose the structuring end of the society or social structure they constitute and delimit—which seek to reconstitute society. As long as the aim of the discriminated against minority ("Bs") is for recognition as an "other," the variability of praxis is negated by the non-subversive hybridity of the discriminated against social actor.

5. According to the Structuralism of De Saussure, "[c]hange originates in linguistic performance, in *parole* [(i.e., speech, practice, or event)], not in *la langue* [(formal structure or institutions)], and what is modified are individual elements of the system of realization. Historical changes affect the system in the end, in that the system will adjust to them, make use of the results of historical change, but it is not the linguistic system which produces them" (Culler, 1976, pg., 41). From a phenomenological structural perspective what this means is that the ends to which the structure of society is directed appears to be unchangeable, even though the interpretive-practices amongst individuals and groups are, and may even contradict that appearance. What happens in the end is that institutional regulators attempt to incorporate these differential interpretive-practices in a way to maintain the order of things so that the ends to which society is structured continues to be realizable in spite of the differential practices. In fact, these practices, defined by their relation with the practices of the structure come to delimit the actual structure.

6. This, as André C. Drainville (1995) observes, "is the essence of what Nicos Poulantzas called the political task of transformation" (pg., 57).

7. Whereas at issue for Bourdieu, Sahlins, and Giddens "is the being of *structure* in history and as history" (Sahlins, 1985, pg. 145), Mocombe's approach does not see structure and history as antinomies, and therefore, focuses on the issue of "being" in *a structure of history*, or the predefined and predetermined "lexicons and representations of signification" that attempt to reproduce an aspect of "Being." Transformation in this understanding is in the development of the historical structure as played-out in the interpretive-practices of the "Beings" or subjects of the system. In other words, reproduction is only attempted in the actual use of the structural ideas in "ideological apparatuses." But this is only an attempt, for the ideas, as objectified by those in power, are distorted as a result of the interpretive-practices of irreducibly situated individuals. So what we have is a dynamic structure driven by interpretive-practices within what is already understood of the objectified concepts of those in power positions, who must attempt to appropriate and redirect interpretative-practices that oppose or threaten their symbolic order. In doing so the structure may or may not be transformed, for transformation rests *only* in the ability of those with contradictory understandings of the symbolic order (Bs in the diagrams) to reconstitute society based on their understanding. As long as, power (As) is able to appropriate and reinflect their (Bs) understanding, reproduction, and as such structural domination along the same structural line (horizontal axis), is the only necessary outcome.

Chapter Three

The Constitution of Modernity and Modern American Society via the Protestant Ethic and the Spirit of Capitalism

Applying Mocombe's phenomenological structural model to the constitution of modernity, the argument here is that the constitution of modernity, as constituted in the American nation-state and the contemporary Protestant capitalist world-system, is the ready-to-hand, unready-to-hand, and present-at-hand by-product of the structuralizing and differentiating effects of the Protestant ethic and the spirit of capitalism, via agricultural, industrial, and postindustrial modes of production, language, ideology, and ideological apparatuses, initially, by the practical consciousness or social class language game of religious, rich, white, Protestant, heterosexual, bourgeois, men in their, unready-to-hand, rejection of the class division and social relations of production of the Catholic feudal order beginning in the sixteenth century. It is within the structural reproduction and differentiating affects of the social class language game of the Protestant Ethic and the spirit of capitalism of European whites that black African consciousness in the US, UK, and the diaspora would become constituted ready-to-hand, unready-to-hand, and present-at-hand.

The God of Judaism "was active in history and in current political events rather than in the primordial sacred time of myth" (Armstrong, 1993, pg. 211). Be that as it may, the traditions of Christianity and Islam inherited this sociohistorical metaphysical understanding of God, which made their central motif a confrontation or a personal meeting between God and humanity devoted to ensuring that God's will is done on earth as it is in heaven:

> This God is experienced as an imperative to action; he calls us to himself; gives us the choice of rejecting or accepting his love and concern. This God relates to human beings by means of a dialogue rather than silent contemplation. He utters a Word, which becomes the chief focus of devotion and which has to be painfully incarnated in the flawed and tragic conditions of earthly life. In Christianity, the most personalized of the three, the relationship with God is characterized by love. But the point of love is that the ego has, in some sense, to be annihilated (Armstrong, 1993, pgs., 210-211).

The barbarian tribes from Europe that eventually brought down the Holy Roman Empire in the fifth century of the common era transmogrified the orientalism and aforementioned historical understanding of Christianity highlighted by Karen Armstrong to fit with their calculating, crude, and barbarous existence, which would subsequently become embodied, once they converted to Christianity, in the discourse and discursive practices of the Protestant Ethic and the spirit of capitalism.

The fall of the Holy Roman Empire would coincide with the rise of imperial Christianity, which began with the evangelism and feudalism of the Roman Catholic Church. The Catholic Church, following Constantine's usurpation of Christianity from the margins of the Roman Empire the fourth century of the Common Era, sought to imperially convert the world's social actors, and constitute the city of God on earth via, the family, church, feudalism and the aristocratic demeanor. Following the Protestant Reformation of the fifteenth and sixteenth centuries, they would subsequently be displaced by the imperial Christianity of the American nation-state embodied in its discourse and discursive practice, the Protestant Ethic and the spirit of capitalism, by the heteronormativity or social class language game of rich, white, Protestant, heterosexual men.

Beginning in the sixteenth century of the common era, God's will on earth was no longer constituted around the family, church, and feudalism of the Catholic Church, but became interpreted as a Hobbesian imperative material struggle of" all against all" in the "flawed and tragic conditions of earthly life" wherein the most pious and egoless souls, which God calls to himself, who accept him, obtained material wealth as a sign of their personal salvation and God's grace and mercy. Protestant reformers such as the Puritans and Pilgrims zealously sought to convert all of Europe and the known world to their Protestant interpretation of the gospel of Jesus via the social class language game of the patriarchal family, Protestant churches, the modern state, class division, and social relations of mercantile and agricultural capitalist production. Their inability to constitute the city of God or their social class language game in Europe, based on their Protestantism, led to their persecution and the eventual founding of the American nation-state as the city of God grounded in the imperial Christianity of the Protestant Ethic and spirit of capitalism. This Protestant Ethic and the spirit of capitalism, which would zealously and imperially seek to displace the evangelism and feudal discourse and discursive practice of the Catholic Church, the Amerindian world worldviews, Islam, African tribalism, etc., via the patriarchal family, Protestant churches, education, the state, and capitalist relations of production, has nothing to do with the egalitarianism, compassion, and social altruistic message of Jesus as highlighted in the synoptic gospels and the gospel of John of the Catholic Church, however. Quite the reverse, it fosters class division, inequality, selfishness, self-interested individualism, and materialism reified, present-at-hand, initially in the discourse and discursive practices, social class language game, of a patriarchal, heterosexual, white male Protestantism and the spirit of capitalism, which discriminated against and marginalized all other practical consciousnesses or ways of organizing and constituting society and the world via the patriarchal family, protestant discourse of churches, class division, the modern state, and the social relations of mercantile, agricultural, industrial, and post-industrial capitalist productions.

Hence with the rise to power of Western European tribes and their Protestant interpretations of Christianity over feudal aristocratic Catholic dogma, the class division and social relations of production of the Protestant ethic and the spirit of capitalism and not the egalitarian, compassionate, and social altruistic message of Jesus, as Max Weber (1958) points out, represents what was understood, the set of values—rationality, hard work, economic gain as a sign of one's predestination, systematic use of time, and a strict asceticism with respect to worldly pleasures and goods—which he claims gave rise to the contemporary capitalist practices that constitute modern societies, and thus American capitalist society, and the existing configuration of bureaucratic power relations, social class language game, within which modern social identity and practical consciousness developed.

The purposive-rationality of these Protestant ideas and practices, mediated and overdetermined by the concepts of class, race, and nation, in other words, historicized social positions, based on racial, national identity, and economic gain for its own sake (class) through the accumulation of capital or profit in a "calling," initially mercantile, agricultural, and industrial relations of production, by which social actors or subjects were differentiated and subjugated (predestined or capitalists/damned or laborers) in the society and the world. Rich, white, heterosexual men universalized their ideology, through ideological apparatuses, the patriarchal family, church, the modern state, class division, and the social relations of production, against all other practical consciousnesses, African polygamous tribalism, homosexuality, etc., arrived at through the deferment of meaning in ego-centered communicative discourse; the drives of the body; and or impulses of subatomic particle. From the late seventeenth century to the present, the ideology and ideological apparatuses of the modern state, family, church, and education, class division, and the social relations of production enframed by the Protestant ethic and spirit of capitalism of rich, white, heterosexual, Protestant, men would be the structure within which social identities were constituted, differentiated, discriminated against, and marginalized.

This theoretical framework differs from both Marxist and non-Marxist structural interpretations of the constitution of modern society in that it begins with the socioreligious cultural (ideal) conceptions that initially structured the social integrative practices that gave rise to the society, while the Marxist and neo-Marxist schools derive the terms from which they begin their analysis from the (material) social relations of production. These two viewpoints, systems and social integration, as our structural Marxist/Weberian approach implies, are inextricably linked, however, and represents the relational structural-cultural framework organized around social relations of production, class division, and the modern state and its ideology and ideological apparatuses, which determined social identity and practices in modern societies. In other words, although philosophically we are able to think these two approaches apart as idealism and materialism, they are not necessarily entirely separable in reality.

Weber defines a capitalistic economic action,

> . . . as one which rests on the expectation of profit by the utilization of opportunities for exchange, that is on (formally) peaceful chances of profit. Acquisition by force (formally and actually) follows its own particular laws, and it is not expedient, however little one can forbid this, to place it in the same category with action which is, in the last analysis, oriented to profits from exchange. Where capitalist acquisition is rationally pursued, the corresponding action is adjusted to calculations in terms of capital. This means that the action is adapted to a systematic utilization of goods or personal services as means of acquisition in such a way that, at the close of a business period, the balance of the enterprise in money assets (or, in the case of a continuous enterprise, the periodically estimated money value of assets) exceeds the capital, i.e. [,] the estimated value of the material means of production used for acquisition in exchange (Weber, 1958, pgs., 17-18).

Although this relationship appears paradoxical, since protestant beliefs did not embrace the idea of economic gain for its own sake,

> Weber's argument is that the rational pursuit of the ultimate values of the ascetic Protestantism characteristic of sixteenth-and seventeenth-century Europe led people to engage in disciplined work; and that disciplined and rational organization of work as a duty is the characteristic feature of modern capitalism—its unique ethos or spirit (Marshall, 1998, pgs., 534).

Thus,

The crucial link to Protestantism comes through the latter's notion of the calling of the faithful to fulfil their duty to God in the methodical conduct of their everyday lives. This theme is common to the beliefs of the Calvinist and neoCalvinist churches of the Reformation. Predestination is also an important belief, but since humans cannot know who is saved (elect) and who is damned, this creates a deep inner loneliness in the believer. In order therefore to create assurance of salvation, which is itself a sure sign (or proof) of election, diligence in one's calling (hard work, systematic use of time, and a strict asceticism with respect to worldly pleasures and goods) is highly recommended— so-called 'this-worldly asceticism'. In general terms, however, the most important contribution of Protestantism to capitalism was the spirit of rationalization that it encouraged. The relationship between the two is deemed by Weber to be one of elective affinity (Marshall, 1998, pg., 535).

The affinity between the Protestantism of a sect and their purposive-rational actions, as we understand Weber to be saying, gave rise to the *economic* organization of modern society, systems integration, as the social psychological practices and ego-ideals (rationally calculating individuals attempting to prove their predestination reflected in their economic gains) of a form of Protestantism, social integration, were rationally and purposively incorporated into the physical world through the bureaucratic organization of the material resource framework around ideological apparatuses, the patriarchal family, church, schools, state, and economy, social relations of production, in order to direct and constitute the identity and practices of social actors and societies for economic gain at the expense of the damned. (In some instances, as in the attempt of the Puritans to usurp power and takeover the English nation-state of the seventeenth century under Oliver Cromwell, bureaucratic means or structural practices (purposive-formal-rational action to organize the lived world) were established around already existing material elements which were re-conceptualized by the sect of rich, white, Protestant, men to foster a society based on wealth, economic gain or capital accumulation as a sign of their salvation and blessings in the eyes of God and others).

Thus, the sociohistorical logic here is that following the Protestant Reformations of the fifteenth and sixteenth centuries, as rich, white, heterosexual Protestant men and their ethos encountered social problems in their attempt to reconfigure or reconstitute sixteenth and seventeenth century European catholic feudal governments, mode of production, ideology, and ideological apparatuses, along the lines of their social class language game, Protestantism and capitalist social relations of production, they became a discriminated against "other" (Puritans, Pilgrims, Calvinists, Lutherans, etc.) minority in the Feudal (catholic) social structure of Europe of the middle ages. Subsequently, these newly created and marginalized "others" left Europe and re-formulated society, in the form of the American social structure by recursively reorganizing and reproducing their "other" Protestant form of being-in-the-world, i.e. Protestantism and the spirit of capitalism, via the organization of the state and its ideological apparatuses, family, church, and schools, class division, and social relations of production, i.e., mercantile, agricultural, industrial, and subsequently postindustrial beginning in the 1970s.

The rules of conduct and ideological apparatuses of the new American society, in other words, were formulated to facilitate the relational logic, ends (substantive rationality), of their, rich, white, heterosexual Protestant men, form of Protestantism, individualism, humanitarianism, rationalism, economic gain, or loss, as a sign of one's election or "damned-ness" in a particular "calling," mercantile, agricultural, industrial, and postindustrial capital, which "embedded" social or cultural relations in what became the modern American political-economic system. With this unready-to-hand and present-at-hand sociohistorical conversion, within the Westphalian nation-state system, of Western society in general and American society in particular, from a catholic feudal social order to a Protestant capitalist social order through the purposive-rationality or social class language game of rich, white, heterosexual Protestant men against all other forms of being-in-the-world, the Protestant ethic became an allowed religion of the society, and thus the "metaphysical" ideas of the Protestant Church became joined with the power and discursive practices of the American Protestant nation-state government as organized around ideological apparatuses, the family, church, school, state, class division, and work or the social relations of production. This "invisible" marriage of church and state led to the formation of the "visible" universal ideals/ideologies (liberalism, democracy, individualism, bourgeois classism, and nationalism) of the American nation-state under god to direct the material economic practices of all social actors, and over time caused the American nation-state/government to refine its doctrine and develop its structure in a way that best served its purposive-rational end, economic gain as a sign of the country and its citizens' salvation and predestination in mercantile, agricultural, industrial, and postindustrial social relations of production, within the emerging global (colonial) economic world-system, which they would gain control of following World War II through transnational ideological apparatuses such as the World Bank (WB), International Monetary Fund (IMF), United Nations (UN), etc.

In materialist terms, the endless accumulation of economic gain, capital, or profit by rich white heterosexual Protestant men became "the defining characteristic and *raison d' être* of this [social] system," which over time pushed "towards the commodification of everything, the absolute increase of world production, and a complex and sophisticated social division of labor based on class" or the amount of capital (economic gain) one had accumulated (Balibar and Wallerstein, 1991, pg., 107). As Jürgen Habermas concludes of this process by which the integrative substantive-rationality of a form of

Protestantism, "the spirit of capitalism," came to dominate modern times by the systemic purposive-rational action of its power agents:

> ... economic production is organized in a capitalist manner, with rationally calculating entrepreneurs [(the predestined prosper)]; public administration is organized in a bureaucratic manner, with juristically trained, specialized officials—that is, they are organized in the form of private enterprises and public bureaucracies. The relevant means for carrying out their tasks are concentrated in the hands of owners and leaders; membership in these organizations is made independent of ascriptive properties [(today, maybe, but not the case for this type of society's early formation)]. By these means, organizations gain a high degree of internal flexibility and external autonomy. In virtue of their efficiency, the organizational forms of the capitalist economy and the modern state administration establish themselves in other action systems to such an extent that modern societies fit the picture of "a society of organizations," even from the standpoint of lay members (Habermas, 1987 [1981], pg., 306).

In this understanding of the origins and organizational basis of modernity and its paragon modern American capitalist society, where "the cultural struggle for distinction is intricately connected to the economic distribution of material goods, which it both legitimates and reproduces" (Gartman, 2002, pg., 257), Weber's explanation, as Jürgen Habermas points out,

> ... refers in the first instance not to the establishment of the labor markets that turned abstract labor power into an expense in business calculations, but to the "spirit of capitalism," that is, to the mentality characteristic of the purposive-rational economic action of the early capitalist entrepreneurs. Whereas Marx took the mode of production to be the phenomenon in need of explanation, and investigated capital accumulation as the new mechanism of system integration, Weber's view of the problem turns the investigation in another direction. For him the explanans is the conversion of the economy and state administration over to purposive-rational action orientations; the changes fall in the domain of forms of social integration. At the same time, this new form of social integration made it possible to institutionalize the money mechanism, and thereby new mechanisms of system integration (Habermas, 1987 [1981], pg., 313).

These two analytic levels, systems and social integration, are not separate if the understanding of the constitution of modernity is understood through our (building on the work of Mocombe) structural and organizational logic. The argument from this Althusserian structural position is that the "predestined" white Protestant entrepreneurial males, a once marginalized group in pre-modern or feudal (catholic) Europe, by re-conceptualizing and maintaining the control of the then feudal market and state within the mythical realities or social class language game of their heterosexual bourgeois male Protestantism, reified their Protestant "practical consciousness" with the state and its ideological apparatuses, family, church, schools, etc. This Protestant metaphysical cultural value or ideology, in other words, they rationalized, present-at-hand, with reality and existence as such, in institutions or ideological apparatuses, the family, church, schools, capitalist global market economy and bourgeois state, operating "through materialized metaphors beyond logical or empirical proof, on ungroundable premises, on nonobservable substances" (Friedland, 2002, pg., 384), in order to mechanically and systemically constitute the identity and direct the agential moments or purposive-rationality of all social actors of the world for the sole purpose of accumulating economic gain (Marx's "capital accumulation") as a sign of their election or progress in the world against those who either were damned as revealed by their poverty in the social relations of production of the society, or conceived of other practical consciousnesses arrived at through the deferment of meaning in ego-centered communicative action.

Class division and the organization of work, mercantile, agricultural, industrial, and postindustrial, for economic gain or profit in modern society was mechanically constituted as white Protestant heterosexual males believing themselves to be "predestined" came as a social class to militarily dominate and control the ontological security of the world and its people of color, who, within their social class language game, they interpellated as the irrational damned or laborers working in the aforementioned social relations of production, through subsequently global institutions or ideological apparatuses like the Protestant churches, schools, the IMF, World Bank, United Nations, etc., in order to (re) produce economic gain for those (predestined) who owned the means and modes of work or production. To put the matter simply, the logic here is that "the spirit of capitalism," which is characteristic of modernity in general and American society in particular, is the socioreligious discursive practice or purposive rationality (mythopraxis) of a form of cultural Protestantism that gave rise to the class identity of social actors, who became differentiated by class, race, and sexual divisions and their social behavioral (methodical) relation to the means and mode of work in modern societies.

The metaphysics of the Protestant Ethic as initially interpreted by rich, white, Protestant men, in other words, structured, through ideology and ideological apparatuses, the physical material world wherein individual social relations and actions were constituted and (re) produced through the organization of work, the modern state, class division, and the praxis of capitalist relations of production through which they, present-at-hand, constituted a heterosexual, patriarchal, white bourgeois social structure reproduced and differentiated by class division and social relations of production.

Thus, the Enlightenment project or attempt to constitute society based on democratically arrived at rational rules of conduct which are sanctioned which began in the seventeenth century with philosophers and artists never materialized as rich, white, heterosexual, bourgeois Protestant males, the emerging power elites of the seventeenth century, incorporated the products of reason and rationality itself into their Protestant metaphysics or social class language game so as to facilitate their purposive socioreligious rationale of economic gain via class division and capitalist relations of production. So it is not that modernity and the organization of the contemporary social world under the hegemony of the American nation-state represents the ever-increasing rationalization of the world, which dates from the Enlightenment. Instead, it represents the ever-increasing mystification of the world around the discursive practices, mythopraxis, or social class language game of the Protestant Ethic and the spirit of capitalism. The reason and rationality of the scientific method, which comes out of the Enlightenment project, was not constituted as a distinct social class language game to direct society under the leadership of scientists and philosophers; instead, the rational-empiricism that would come to dominate the seventeenth century became a facilitator for promoting the ethos of an emerging Protestantism and the spirit of capitalism reified in the discourse and discursive practices of the nation-state and its ideological apparatuses, i.e., education, church, family, etc., and organization of work or social relations of production under the leadership and social class language games of rich, white, Protestant, heterosexual men.

Hence, the Americentric dominated form of modernity, neoliberalism with its emphasis on family life, individuality, education, class division, free markets, free trade, political and economic liberalism, outsourcing of jobs, privatization, etc., which contemporarily dominates the world in and through the discourse of (neoliberal) globalization represents the continual attempt to homogenize and universalize social identities and social practices the world over to fit within the metaphysical discourse and discursive practices of agents of the Protestant Ethic who purposively rationalized the discourse of their metaphysic into the laws and practices of their society and global institutions against the metaphysics of adherents of the Enlightenment, the poor, and other metaphysical systems. Hence, the mythical realities of rich, white, Protestant, heterosexual bourgeois males canonized, present-at-hand, in laws and social institutions determined their praxis, and relationally attempted to determine the praxis of all "others" they encountered in their quest to prove their predestination. It should also be mentioned that modern societies in the global economic world-system, as all became interpellated as owners and workers, itself became a dialectical totality that underwent reproduction and transformation based on internal contradictions and class differentiation based upon capital accumulation motivated by the desire to acquire capital or economic gain for its own sake as prescribed by the substantive-rationality or social class language game of the Protestant Ethic and the spirit of capitalism (Balibar and Wallerstein, 1991; Smith, 1996). In fact, the modern political and economic ideologies of liberalism, conservatism, and radicalism are grounded in, and can be deduced from, the metaphysics of "the Protestant Ethic and the spirit of capitalism": radicalism representing a revolutionary response against the ideals and practices of liberal bourgeois heterosexual white male Protestantism that included bourgeois technical rationality, individualism, class inequality, racialism, and heterosexism; conservatism, representing strict commitment to its ideologies of individualism, class inequality, heterosexism, religiosity, and racialism; and liberalism was deduced from the Christian (Protestant) ethic of individual humanism, rationalism, anti-dogmatism, classism, and the liberal democratic capitalist state's ability to foster that ethic.

GLOBALIZATION

From the sixteenth century to the present, the differentiating effects of the Protestant Ethic and the spirit of capitalism under the leadership of rich, white, Protestant, heterosexual men became the structural framework or social class language game within which all peoples of the world were interpellated and embourgeoised via language, ideology, ideological apparatuses of the nation-state, and mode of production. The contemporary phenomenon of globalization is the continuing attempt, under the leadership of an embourgeoised hybrid, multiracial, multisexual, multinational, etc., upper-class of owners and high-level executives, who in the 1960s sought, unready-to-hand, equality of opportunity, recognition, and distribution with their white counterparts, to structure the world within the structural metaphysics or social class language game of the Protestant Ethic and the spirit of capitalism against other practices and organizations of realities arrived at through the deferment in ego-centered communicative discourse. Contemporarily, "culture of globalization" and the "globalization as culture" metaphors represent two sociological approaches to understanding the contemporary post-modern phenomenon we call globalization under American hegemony (1970s-2000s). These two sociopolitical understandings regarding the origins and nature of globalization, as Kevin Archer et al (2007) points out, have "set off a vigorous and at times rancorous debate within the social sciences" (pg. 2). On one side of the debate you have theorists who emphasize the "culture of globalization" and argue the idea that "the constitutive role of culture is critical for grasping the continued hegemony of capitalism in the form of globalization . . . Culture, they assert is increasingly being co-opted and deployed as a new accumulation strategy to broaden and deepen the frontiers of capitalism and to displace its inherent crisis tendencies" (Archer, 2007, pgs. 2-3). In a word, in the continual hegemonic quest of capitalism to equalize the conditions of the world to serve capital, globalization, in the eyes of "culture of globalization" theorists, represents a stage of capitalism's development highlighted by the commodification of culture as a means for accumulating profits from the purchasing and consuming power of a transnational class of administrative bourgeoisies and professional cosmopolitan elites in core, semi-periphery, and periphery nation-states who subscribe to the social integrative norms of liberal bourgeois Protestantism (hard work, economic gain, political and economic liberalism, consumption, etc.).

In other words, the material and symbolic cultural elements of the cultures of the world are commodified by the upper class of owners and high-level executives of core countries—where finance capital and service jobs predominate—to make a profit or produce surplus-value—given the declining significance of profit from industrial production that have been shipped or outsourced to semi-periphery and periphery nations giving rise to their national bourgeoisies whose cultural practices and tastes have been nationalized—by fulfilling the consumption tastes of the financiers, administrative bourgeoisies, professional classes, and cosmopolitan elites of nation-states throughout the world who control their masses as a surplus labor force for global capital. Globalization, therefore, is the integration of the cultural realm and individual experiences into the commodity chains of the capitalist elites, who homogenize, through the media and other "ideological state apparatuses," the behavior and tastes of global social actors as consumers thereby homogenizing the cultural practices and tastes of the middle and under class peoples of the world in order to generate profit in postindustrial economies such as the US and UK.

This "culture-of-globalization" understanding of globalization or the postmodern condition in late capitalist development is a well-supported position, which highlights, in the twenty-first century, the continued hegemony of capitalism or capitalist relations of production in the form of globalization (Hardt and Negri, 2000; Kellner, 1988; Giddens, 1991; Harvey, 1989, 1990; Jameson, 1984, 1991). This line of thinking, in which theorists point to the underlining drive of globalization as the continuing historical push to socially, economically, and politically (under) develop the rest of the world along the lines, or as a simulacrum, of Western American and European Societies to facilitate capital accumulation, began with European colonialism, continued through the "development project" of the Cold-war era, and now is embodied in the globalization process. This historical process is highlighted in modernization, development, dependent development, world-systems theories, and contemporarily it is a trend outlined in the theoretical works of postmodern theorists such as David Harvey (1989, 1990) and Fredric Jameson (1984, 1991) who view globalization as postmodern or the cultural logic of late capitalist development in core or developed countries. "Culture of globalization" theorists, such as Harvey and Jameson, therefore, view globalization as the new initiative, with the same intentions, replacing the accumulation and modernization project of colonialism and development.

The homogenization, accumulation, and "modernization" project in European colonialism operated through the establishment of either colonies of settlement, "which often eliminate[d] indigenous people," or rule, where colonial administrators reorganize[d] existing cultures by imposing new inequalities [(around class, gender, race, and caste)] to facilitate their exploitation, wherein an unequal division of agricultural (monoculture) labor was physically and psychologically forced upon the peoples of color the world over to sustain the industrial and manufacturing cultural life of Europeans, while simultaneously disrupting, destroying, and reconfiguring the cultural practices and tastes of the colonized peoples within the binary (structural) logic of the (European) colonizer (McMichael, 2008, pg. 27). As Philip McMichael (2008, pg. 31) observed of the European colonization process,

> From the sixteenth century, European colonists and traders traveled along African coasts to the New World and across the Indian Ocean and the China seas seeking fur, precious metals, slave labor, spices, tobacco, cacao, potatoes, sugar, and cotton. The principal European colonial powers—Spain, Portugal, Holland, France, and Britain—and their merchant companies exchanged manufactured goods such as cloth, guns, and implements for these products and for Africans taken into slavery and transported to the Americas. In the process, they reorganized the world.
>
> The basic pattern was to establish in the colonies specialized extraction and production of raw materials and primary products that were unavailable in Europe. In turn, these products fueled European manufacturing as industrial inputs and foodstuffs for its industrial labor force. On a world scale, this specialization between European economies and their colonies came to be termed the colonial division of labor.
>
> While the colonial division of labor stimulated European industrialization, it forced non-Europeans into primary commodity production. Specialization at each end of the exchange set in motion a transformation of social and environmental relationships, fueled by a dynamic relocation of resources and energy from colony to metropolis: an unequal ecological exchange. Not only were the colonies converted into exporters of raw materials and foodstuffs, but also they became "exporters of sustainability."

The sociocultural outcome of this exploitative and oppressive socioeconomic military system was a racialized social structural relationship relationally constituted based on the "unequal" colonial division of labor and "unequal" ecological exchanges, which divided the social actors of the world between white, Christian, civilized, and "developed" European colonizers (masters) whose "burden" was to civilize and (under) develop the "undeveloped," "backward," non-European, colonized, colored, other, "heathens" (slaves) of the world. This European civilizing of the non-European colored "heathens" of the world initially took place through the Christian churches of the West, whose biblical tenets and metaphysics were used to justify the master/slave relationship of colonialism as well as teach its work ethic, which eventually homogenized the social actions of social actors to benefit the white male power elites of an emerging gendered, racialized, and religious global capitalist world-system that developed the white colonizer, while simultaneously underdeveloping the colored colonized who were systematically forced to become agents of the Protestant ethic in agricultural production.

The end of the socioeconomic military colonial system in the form of decolonization in the twentieth century did not end the colonizer/colonized relational relationship, but gave rise to a new nation-state system of civilizing, domination, and exploitation within the hegemony of this emerging gendered, racialized, and religious global capitalism. Decolonization gave birth to what Philip McMichael calls, "the development project." According to McMichael, "[t]he mid-twentieth century development project (1940s-1970s), an internationally orchestrated program of national economic growth, with foreign financial, technological, and military assistance under the conditions of the Cold War, managed the aftermath of collapsing European and Japanese empires within the idealistic terms of the United nations and its focus on [national-state] governments implementing a human rights-based social contract with their citizens . . . to equalize conditions across the world in laying the foundations of a global market that progressively overshadowed the states charged with development in the initial post-World War II era" (McMichael, 2008, pg., 21). Hence, the development project from the postcolonial era to the 1970s emphasized and continued the "unequal" colonial division of labor and "unequal" ecological exchanges within an Americentric dominated capitalist world-system subdivided into three geopolitical segments to benefit capitalist accumulation: the First World, the developed capitalist Western countries plus Japan with America the model for development; the Second World comprised of Communist Soviet blocs; and the Third World comprised of postcolonial bloc of nations.

Whereas under colonialism, as McMichael notes, "[t]he basic pattern was to establish in the colonies specialized extraction and production of raw materials and primary products that were unavailable in Europe. In turn, these products fueled European manufacturing as industrial inputs and foodstuffs for its industrial labor force" (31), in the development phase of postcolonial capitalism, the process was reversed as the First World sought to take advantage of the desire of the postcolonial elites of the Third World to develop their nation-states along the lines of the industrial First World. The basic global pattern was to establish in the emerging postcolonial "Third-World" nation-states specialized manufacturing and industrial production sites that were outsourced from the First World. In turn, the outsourcing of these manufacturing and industrial jobs by the First World to take advantage of the urban underemployment and low-wage economy caused by the deagriculturalization of Third World countries fueled First World, especially American, agribusinesses that channeled food surpluses, under a "food-aid-regime," to Third World countries. "In agriculture, the Third World's share of world agricultural exports fell from 53 to 31 percent between 1950 and 1980, while the American granary consolidated its critical role in world agricultural trade. By the 1980s, the United States was producing 17 percent of the world's wheat, 63 percent of its corn, and 63 percent of its soybean; its share of world exports was 36 percent in wheat, 70 percent in corn, and 59 percent in soybeans" (McMichael, 2008, pgs., 67-68). What developed from this global economic relationship was that Third World industrialization outlined by W.W. Rostow's stages of development fueled First world economic growth agriculturally and technologically, while underdeveloping some Third World countries, and dependently developing others within the capitalist global world-system, hence recolonizing the Third World as they became indebted given their need to import food to feed their populous.

The postcolonial nations had no say in this new "unequal" development paradigm as "decisions about postcolonial political arrangements were made in London and Paris where the colonial powers, looking to sustain spheres of influence, insisted on the nation-state as the only appropriate political outcome of decolonization" (McMichael, 2008, pg., 47). Be that as it may, "[t]his new paradigm inscribed First World power and privilege in the new institutional structure of the postwar international economy. In the context of the Cold War between First and Second Worlds (for the hearts and resources of the ex-colonial world), "development" was simultaneously the restoration of a capitalist world market to sustain First World wealth, through access to strategic natural resources, and the opportunity for Third World countries to emulate First World civilization and living standards" (McMichael, 2008, pg., 45). The "development project," In this way, as McMichael further observed, continued the hegemony of capitalism, which started with colonialism, through the universalization of a global market system driven by the nation-state and economic growth through agricultural and industrial productions (2008, pg., 46). Globalization (1970s-2000s) is a continuation of this hegemonic capitalist process in a post-communist world.

Globalization under American capitalist hegemony seeks to dismantle the state-centered exploitation of colonial and development capitalism via the invisible hand of economic (neo) liberalism, education, class division, and social relations of global production. "The globalization project (1970s-2000s)," as McMichael observes, "liberalizing trade and investment rules, and privatizing public goods and services, has privileged corporate rights over the social contract and redefined development as a private undertaking" (2008, pg., 21). That is to say, in reestablishing a global capitalist economy through the development project that followed colonialism, the First World was able to indebt Third World countries through an export-oriented industrialization that fueled the wealth of First World agribusinesses, transnational corporations, and their citizens who became consumers of inexpensive manufactured goods from the Third World. Hence, "[e]xport-oriented industrialization fueled rapid economic growth, legitimizing a new 'free market' model of development, and in the 1980s this was represented as the solution to the debt crisis [of Third World countries]. Development, which had been defined as nationally managed economic growth, was redefined in the World Bank's *World Development Report 1980* as 'participation in the world market'" (McMichael, 2008, pg., 117). This global market is controlled and directed by multinational and transnational corporations operating in First World postindustrial cities where high finance banking jobs and low-end service jobs predominate over manufacturing and industrial jobs that have been outsourced to semi-periphery or developing nations. What has developed in turn is a continuation of the tripartite system of the development phase. In the globalization phase, however, what has developed is a tripartite system in which the global economic system parallels Immanuel Wallerstein's world-systems conception: a periphery group of poor nations whose comparative advantage is agricultural production and tourism; a semi-periphery group of industrial based nations, i.e., India, Mexico, Brazil, South Africa, and China; and a postindustrial group of core or developed nations led by the United States of America who generate profit by servicing the cultural consumptive needs of a multicultural and multiethnic transnational capitalist class who control and monitor their (US and other core countries) investments in periphery and semi-periphery nations.

In other words, the contemporary (1970 to the present) post-industrial mode of production in developed (core) states like the US is no longer characterized or driven by the industrial means for accumulating capital, which dominated the social relations of production of the last one hundred years in core or developed nations, instead, the present globalization condition is driven-by, post-industrialism (consumerism)—the new means for accumulating capital—, and in such "developed" societies like the U.S., Europe, and Japan, is characterized not by the industrial organization of labor, which have been outsourced overseas, but rather by capitalist finance and service occupations catering to the consumerist demands of a dwindling (transnational, transcultural, transracial, etc.) middle class the world over. In short, the rate of economic gain for its own sake or profit has fallen in industrial production due to labor laws (products of the welfare state) and ecological cost in developed countries like the US; hence the practice now among investors operating out of the US and other developed nations is on financial expansion "in which 'over-accumulated' capital switches from investments in production and trade, to investments in finance, property titles, and other claims on future income" (Trichur, 2005, pg., 165).

On a global scale, the bifurcation defining this current conjuncture is characterized on the one hand by an expansion of industrial production into some (others remain agricultural producers) developing or periphery countries, i.e., the semi-periphery, where the rate of labor exploitation has risen given their lack of environmental and labor laws, devalued labor, and the dismantling of the welfare state; and on the other hand, consumerism of cheaply produced goods and high-end service occupations has come to dominate developed and developing societies as capital in the developed world seeks to allow and incorporate, through the commodification of their cultural identities, the transnational class of elite "others" who administer the assets of capital into their consumption patterns. Archer et al (2007) sum up the nature of this position brilliantly,

> . . . since the mid-1990s, the application of GATS ([General Agreement on Trade in Services)] has slowly but surely led to a redefinition of culture primarily if not exclusively within the parameters of neo-liberal capitalism. The presumption is that flourishing cultures go hand-in-glove with flourishing capitalism . . . .[t]his strategic articulation and subordination of culture to the requirements of capitalism is what has been called 'cultural capitalism' . . . .This line of thinking is best exemplified by David Harvey . . . and to a lesser extent by Fredric Jameson . . . himself. These theorists have launched an unrelenting critique of cultural capitalism as a 'carnival for the elite' which enables politicians and policymakers to conceal growing socio-spatial inequalities, polarizations, and distributional conflicts between the haves and the have-nots. This critique is further underscored by their dismissal of culture as nothing more than a tool for economic regeneration through the 'mobilization of the spectacle' . . . , because the tourist and entertainment city requires the urban spectacle to reinforce place-marketing and residential development . . . .In short, for this group, culture is just another commodity available for consumption in the world's supermarkets (3).

"Globalization-as-culture" theorists out rightly reject this socioeconomic position or interpretation underlying the processes of globalization. They believe "that globalization is marked by the hollowing out of national cultural spaces either consequent upon the retrenchment of the nation state or because culture continues to be a relatively autonomous sphere" (Archer et al, 2007, pg., 2). That is, "[f]or the "globalization-as-culture" group . . . culture is not that easily enjoined due to its inherent counter-hegemonic properties vis-à-vis neo-liberal globalization. Rather, for this group . . . , contemporary globalization is not merely economic, but a system of multiple cultural articulations which are shaped by disjunctive space-time coordinates. In other words, globalization is as much if not more the product of inexorable and accelerated migratory cultural flows and electronic mass mediations beyond the space-time envelopes of the nation-state system and the successive socio-spatial fixes of global capitalism" (Archer et al, 2007, pg.,

4). In fact, culture, in many instances, serves as a counter-hegemonic movement to (neo) liberal capitalism as a governing "rational" system. This line of thinking is best exemplified in the works of Stuart Hall (1992), John Tomlinson (1999), Homi Bhabha (1994), and Edward Said (1993) among many others. For these theorists cultural exchanges are never one-dimensional, and hybridization of culture in many instances serves as a counter-hegemonic force to the homogenization processes of global capital.

Theoretically, this debate between the advocates of the "globalization-as-culture" and the "culture-of-globalization" hypotheses we argue here is a fruitless debate grounded in a false ontological and epistemological understanding of the origins and nature of the (neo) liberal capitalist system that gives rise to the processes of globalization. Both groups ontologically and epistemologically assume that the origins of capitalism and its discursive practice is grounded in reason and rationality, thus drawing on the liberal distinction between capitalism as a public and neutral system of rationality that stands apart from the understanding of it as a private sphere or lifeworld cultural form grounded in the ontology of the Protestant ethic as argued by Max Weber. The latter position, if assumed by both schools, is a point of convergence that resolves their opposition, and gives a better understanding of the origins and nature of the processes of globalization and counter movements to what are in fact metaphysical cultural forces/social class language games.

Essentially, both schools of thought are putting forth the same convergence argument, the culture of globalization position from a Marxian systems integration perspective and the globalization as culture position from a Weberian social integration perspective. For the culture of globalization position cultural products and practices are homogenized to be integrated within the rational rules or systemicity/social class language game of capitalist relations of production and consumption at the world-system level so as to generate surplus-value from the consumption of cultural products as commodities in core postindustrial nations, industrial production in semi-periphery nations, and agricultural production in periphery nations.

The globalization as cultural group suggests that in the process of acculturating social actors to the organization of work within the capitalist world-system, homogenization does not take place. Instead, in the process of integration within the world-system, cultural groups intersubjectively defer meaning in ego-centered communicative discourse to hybridize the lexicons of significations coming out the globalization process thereby maintaining their cultural forms not in a commodified form but as a class-for-itself seeking to partake in the global community as hybrid social actors governed by the liberal rational logic of the marketplace.

The two positions are not mutually exclusive, however. Globalization contemporarily represents the homogenization of social discourse and action via hybridization. That is globalization represents the discursive practice, "spirit of capitalism," social class language game of agents of the Protestant Ethic seeking to allow for and homogenize "other" human behaviors, cultures, around the globe within the logic of their metaphysical discourse, "The Protestant Ethic and the spirit of capitalism," so as to accumulate profit, via agricultural, industrial, and post-industrial/consumerist production, for the predestined from the damned. That is, via globalization social actors around the globe are socialized via ideological apparatuses, education, class division, and social relations of production, to become agents of the Protestant ethic so as to fulfill their labor and consumption roles in the organization of work, agricultural, industrial, or postindustrial production, required by their states in the global capitalist world-system under American hegemony since World War II. Proper socialization in the contemporary capitalist American dominated world-system is tantamount to hybridization, i.e., a liberal bourgeois Protestant *other* working for those who own the means and forces of production so as they themselves can become bourgeois as profit trickles down from capital operating in the first world or developed countries to the rest of the world, in order to consume the cultural and individual products found in postindustrial world-cities throughout the globe. Hence, hybridization of other cultures, via the homogenization process of globalization, is a simulacrum of white agents of the Protestant ethic, which enables the latter (whites) to make social actors of other cultures known for two reasons, to socialize them to the work ethic of the globalizing process and to accumulate surplus-value as the former service the others of their community for what has become since the 1960s a multicultural, multisexual, multiracial, etc., global capitalist world-system dominated by whites and hybrid others, differentiated by class and their social relations to production, seeking equality of opportunity, recognition, and distribution for the world's poor within the framework of the Protestant Ethic and the spirit of capitalism. Thus in the postindustrial economy of the US and UK identity politics are fostered and allowed to develop through the state, ideological apparatuses, and global social relations of production for capital accumulation. As such identity constitution or the theorizing about identity politics cannot be understood through the notion of the decentered subject or the deferment of meaning in ego-centered communicative action as highlighted in the theorizing of West, Gilroy, hooks, and Collins. But their theoretical assumptions must be understood as derived from the class division and social relations of global production under the leadership of an emerging transnational, multiracial, multicultural, multisexual, etc., upper-class of owners and high-level executives working with whites to co-opt identities arrived-at through the deferment of meaning in ego-centered communicative discourse, drives of the body, and or impulses of subatomic particles into the class division and social relations of production of the Protestant Ethic and the spirit of capitalism.

Put differently, the logic here is that the theories of West, Gilroy, hooks, and Collins regarding the constitution of their own identities in particular and black consciousnesses in general derive from the ideology and class division of neoliberal policies of globalizing capitalist processes under American hegemony and postindustrial capitalist relations of the nation-state. It is the class division and social relations of production coupled with the experience of white American capital with the liberal hybrid black American's struggle for equality of opportunity, recognition, and distribution beginning in slavery and ending in the civil rights movement of the 1960s, which led to the passage of civil rights legislation that integrated blacks into the fabric of the society under the purposive-rationality or social class language game of their liberal black hybrid leadership in the likes of W.E.B. Du Bois, Martin Luther King Jr., Barack Obama, etc., which would come to constitute the contemporary processes of globalization and this adoption of postcolonial, postmodern, and post-structural theory highlighted in the works of Gilroy, West, hooks, and Collins, in other words.

Following the civil rights movement of the 1960s and adoption of civil rights legislation such as the Civil Rights Act of 1964, the experience of white American capital with liberal hybrid blacks would give rise to hybridization as the mechanism of social integration for all ethnic, racial, gender, and other minorities into American postindustrial capitalist relations of production locally and globally. Locally, discrimination was outlawed throughout American society, which in theory became a color-blind multicultural, multiracial, multisexual, etc., postindustrial social setting dictated by the state. Subsequently, the global outsourcing of industrial work by American capital beginning in the 1970s would be coupled with hybridization as the mechanism of social integration for ethnic others into global capitalist relations of production under American hegemony. That is, under the passage of civil rights legislation such as the Civil Rights Act of 1964 to integrate liberal hybrid blacks into the fabric of American society, the American nation-state reinforced its liberal bourgeois Protestantism without regards to race, creed, nationality, sex, religion, etc. With the advent of outsourcing or globalization under American hegemony beginning in the 1970s, other ethnic, racial, gender, and other minorities the world-over were integrated or socialized, like the liberal hybrid black Americans, via ideological apparatuses such as education, the media, Protestant churches, etc., to work for American capital within the framework of this color-blind new world economic order. In the processes of globalization, American capital sought and seeks to hybridize other ethnic cultures the world over via the retrenchment of the nation state and color-blind neoliberal economic legislation in order to make social actors of other cultures known for two reasons: first, to socialize them to the work ethic of the globalizing capitalist social relations of production; and second, to accumulate surplus-value as American capital sought and seeks to service the elite others of ethnic, racial, gender, and other communities as agents of and for capital, i.e., cultural producers, consumers, and administrative bourgeoisie controlling production for global capital, for their postindustrial economy.

Postmodern, postcolonial, and post-structural rhetoric are the academic and political discourses of globalization and postindustrial capitalist relations of production of the contemporary age. As a result of the emergence of a postindustrial capitalism intent on allowing divergent meanings and subjective experiences to emerge around their class positions for capital accumulation in a service economy focused on entertainment and service, non-class meanings and subjective experiences, homosexuality, black feminism, etc., which were, and to some extent continue to be, discriminated against by both the black underclass and bourgeoisie of earlier capitalist relations of production are fostered and allowed to emerge within the dialectic of the global (postindustrial) capitalist social class structure. These non-class meanings and subjective experiences, homosexuality, black feminism, Pan-Africanism, etc., practical consciousnesses, which are the product of the deferment of meaning in ego-centered communicative discourse, contemporarily, are seeking equality of opportunity, recognition, and distribution within the dialectic of a postindustrial capitalist social structure that stratifies and commodifies these non-class identities, meanings, and subjective experiences around their class positions (castes in classes) or social relations to production for capital accumulation in the service economies of core, postindustrial nations, such as the US and UK. What has emerged, as a result, are these, present-at-hand, theories of ambivalence, hybridity, intersectionality, etc., among bourgeois academics highlighting the discourse by which these variant subjective positions have been marginalized and prevented from achieving equality of opportunity, recognition, and distribution within the global (postindustrial) capitalist social structure of class inequality and differentiation of the US , UK, and elsewhere. Be that as it may, by no means can double consciousness, hybridity, intersectionality, etc., be viewed, against the discourse of the pathological-pathogenic, adaptive-vitality, anti-essentialist, and anti-anti-essentialist positions, as the universal mechanism by which black consciousness and communities were constituted as their rhetoric, like black consciousnesses and black communities in the US, UK, and the diaspora are the ready-to-hand, unready-to-hand (because of the discriminatory effects of the social structure), and present-at-hand (as the bourgeoisie attempts to reify their experiences) by-product of the global (industrial and postindustrial) capitalist social structure of class inequality and differentiation, which attempts to structure the practices of subjective experiences within class differentiation and thereby control practice, diversity, and meaning constitution for capital accumulation.

Chapter Four

The Constitution of Black America within the Protestant Ethic and the Spirit of Capitalism

Africans (an estimated 430,000 imported to North America during the whole period of the Atlantic Slave trade)[1] were like Native Americans and many poor whites had "other" forms of orientation in the world distinct from the Protestant form of the American social structure and its agents. The Africans encountered or were brought (1619-1808), ready-to-hand, unready-to-hand, and present-at-hand, into this once marginalized, unready-to-hand, Protestant worldview as marginalized forced laborers and indentured servants in order to satisfy the idea and practice of "economic gain" in agricultural production expropriated from the "damned" for the benefit of the industrially developed "predestined" in urban centers that the new Protestant—global economic—order ("slave-based plantation" agricultural capitalism)[2] proffered. In this ideologically economic driven new symbolic colonial world where the peoples of color of the world were commodified, present-at-hand, as ignorant agricultural workers to sustain the white urbane industrial labor force of Europe and America, however, individual property rights were reconceptualized and elevated to a position sanctioned by divine authority and considered superior to all other rights, including the human rights and life of indigenous peoples, bonded laborers, and those who would eventually be bought as slaves (Smedley, 1999: 53; McMichael, 2008, pg., 21). Thus, the institutional regulators (rich, white, Protestant, male landowners), given the need to maintain and reproduce the then bifurcated agriculturally/industrially based economic stratified order of things among those "others" who did not subscribe to it in order to sustain and maintain the labor force of white industrial workers, rationalized the labor requirements within what was already understood, the purposive-rationality of the Protestant Ethic and the spirit of capitalism. By the time America became a nation-state in the late eighteenth-century this stratification or class differentiation had already been established through the commodification of the African. In the bifurcated colonial order of bureaucratic social structural relations of white Protestantism and agricultural capitalism, Africans became the structurally differentiated undeveloped perpetual "black," non-Protestant, damned agricultural worker (commodity) who worked (as their property) *freely* for the industrially developed predestined white Protestants in order to maximize the rate of profit or economic gain in the colonial global economic system of the seventeenth, eighteenth, and nineteenth centuries.[3]

As the black radical nationalist thinker Maulana Karenga (1993) observed, several material factors made the enslavement of Africans for the increase of the rate of profit or economic gain in agricultural production to sustain the industrial labor force of Europe and America more feasible and permanent than that of other marginalized "damned" groups such as Native Americans and poor white indentured-servants:

> The first factor was Africa's closeness to the Caribbean where plantations were set up early and where Africans were "seasoned," i.e., made manageable, and then re-exported. Secondly, Africans already had experience in large-scale agriculture with their own fields and European plantations in Africa, unlike the Native Americans who mainly hunted and gathered their food. Thirdly, Africans had relative immunity to European diseases due to long-term contact, whereas the Native Americans did not and were decimated at first by this.
>
> Fourthly, the practicality of African enslavement rested in their low escape possibilities as opposed to Native Americans and whites due to unfamiliarity with the land, high social visibility and lack of a nearby home base. Fifthly, there were no major political repercussions for the enslavement of Africans, unlike the Native Americans who had people here to retaliate and the whites whose enslavement would challenge the tenets of Christianity and the age of enlightenment and reason on which Europe prided itself.
>
> Finally, the basis of the American system of enslavement was in its justifiability in European racist thought. Although the enslavement of Africans was based in economic reasons, it also rested in racism as an ideology . . . Racism as an ideology became a justification and encouragement for African enslavement (Karenga, 1993, pgs., 121-122).

These factors, however, were not perceived or conceived from a transcendental Enlightenment vantage point as Karenga's scientized material perspective implied. But their conjunctures were reasoned within what was already understood by those rich, white, Protestant, men in power positions in the society.[4] Their rationalization through the prism of their Protestant ideology or substantive-rationality, social class language game, would come to relationally explain the social organization of the society and the structural framework by which African American practical consciousness was constituted.

The ever-increasing purposive-rationalization of the Protestant Ethic and spirit of capitalism by rich, white, Protestant men progressively elaborated and expanded on ideological themes of Christian brotherhood, human rights, and the elevation of the good of the many over the privileges of the few, which were recursively organized and reproduced through the "secular" practice or purposive-rationality of bourgeois racial, gender, and patriarchal capitalism that would come to constitute American society. The ideas of predestination through economic gain (as a sign of one's election or progress) justified the privileging of the good of the many (who were predestined to succeed—success being reflected in their economic gains or rate of profit) to have dominion over those who were not predestined and who were based on the structural (relational) logic of the former, undeveloped, ungodly, backward, and damned. Within the structural logic and differentiation of this worldview, those Protestants and non-Protestants, who were not predestined, like their predestined counterparts, were uncertain of their plight. They had to work hard in a particular calling for economic gain "as a sign." The enslaved, "damned" Africans, given their physical and behavioral differences, were rationalized in relation to the symbolic signifiers of white Protestantism. Interpellated and embourgeoised in the white Protestant new world order, the Africans were not quite human to the white Protestants given the differences in African pigmentation, irrationalism, promiscuity, barbarity, carelessness, etc., created by their material conditions, and were therefore made to work for the whites. Class, and status position, and one's predestination were reflected in the rate of profit or economic gain obtained from the production of the "damned" and racial typology in class reinforced the belief in predestination.

Rich, Protestant, white, male factory and land owners (the power elites of the society), the "enlightened" and "progressive" predestined, institutionalized or rationalized, present-at-hand, their biblical, cultural, and entrepreneurial values and mysticism into laws and practices, slave codes, miscegenation laws, systematic labor, capitalism, the individualism of civil rights and liberties, patriarchal family, and republicanism. Their values were embedded in laws, treaties, pacts, agreements, the US and state constitutions and came to bureaucratically structure the political economy of the material resource framework within which the society became ensconced. At the same time structural or relational "blackness" and economic "class" developed as social categories (among others) for identity construction. More than anything else, this process of class and "racial"/national differentiation, counterposed as it was by equalization between predestined rich, white, Protestant, men, was responsible for the dialectical totality that gave rise to the black practical consciousnesses that would come to constitute and dominate modern

American society embedded in the social class language game of heterosexual black male bourgeois liberalism.

Hence, the structural position assumed here is that the purposive-rationality of these Protestant laws and practices were utilized in the social institutions ("ideological apparatuses") of family, church, schools, organization of work (indentured servitude and slavery initially, consumerism and wage-labor, presently), etc., to condition or socialize (integrate) the masses—the constituting unit of the social structure—for the sole purpose of work or the reproduction of the American social relations of production, i.e. agricultural production in the South and industry in North. The, ready-to-hand, acceptance and embodiment of these laws and practices gave the masses and the power elites or institutional regulators their practical consciousness or purposive-rationality, while all other forms of social action, arrived at through the deferment of meaning in ego-centered communicative action, drives of the body, impulses of neuronal energies, and the structurally differentiated were marginalized and discriminated against as unequal and "other" by rich, white, Protestant, heterosexual men.

So in this case, the Africans, ninety percent of whom could not read, were introduced (in 1619), ready-to-hand, as a marginalized unit of the structure and "seasoned" in the Protestant doctrines through slave codes, the Protestant churches (initially by white ministers, later on by native-born slaves), slavery, individual civil rights and liberties, etc. Unlike literate non-Protestant and Protestant whites who could work hard and eventually—if predestined—become masters or what amounted to the same thing institutional regulators, the structurally differentiated group of Africans had to accept their prescribed lowly conditions (slaves) given the fact that their physical difference and perpetual "otherness," in relation to white bourgeois (patriarchal) Protestantism, did not allow for their predestination or equality.

The relationship of Africans with the white, heterosexual, Protestant, power elites, therefore, operated along a master/slave relationship where the rich, white, Protestant males (masters) worked and re-worked the ideas and practices of the Protestant Ethic on the one hand and on the other their terms and representations for the Africans' forms (soul-less, blacks, poor, savages and barbarous, less intelligent and human than their white counterparts, ungodly, promiscuous, undeveloped, etc.) of being in the world. The rich, white, Protestant, heterosexual males used the African representations to delimit their own form (godly, pious, urban, obedient, pure, civilized, diligent, intelligent, industrial, etc.) of being in the world and reproduced the colonial social relations of production through agricultural slavery and industrialism.

The Africans initially transported into this global "mechanical solidarity" or social class language game and its differentiating affects in the seventeenth and early part of the eighteenth centuries were different and heterogeneous "others" with distinct practical consciousnesses. As a "ready-to-hand" dominated deployable unit of the white Protestant economic social relations of American society they became a homogeneous group or social class language game, blacks (later differentially stratified along class lines and their adaptive responses to enslavement) prepared for one facet of life in the American social structure, "systematic [agricultural slave] labor" (Blassingame, 1972, pg. 3), conditioned by the obedient work ethic of Protestantism, which was juxtaposed against the industrial urban life and work of whites.

Africans came from all over Africa[5] and embodied different structurally determined subjective forms of being-in-the-world which ranged from rigid patriarchy and traditional Islamic practices to matrilineal polygamous tribalism. By the nineteenth-century (1808), which marks the discontinuation of the African slave trade to the United States, these "other" forms of being-in-the-world were discriminated against and marginalized within the American Protestant social structure. Native-born classified blacks, "the best of the house servants, mulattoes, artisans, and the educated free Negro from the [(industrial)] North," due to their intimacy with whites, freedom, and privileges, served as a reference group for the larger black community. They accepted, embodied, and recursively reorganized and reproduced the Protestant socioreligious cultural work ethos of the society in their material practices and purposive-rationality. Black identity or practical consciousness for them became, in keeping with the ethos of their white counterparts, synonymous with Standard English, Protestantism, development, education, freedom, equality, hard work, wage-labor, and monogamous patriarchal family against the material condition or pathologies, Black English Vernacular, poverty, single female-headed households, emotionalism, promiscuity, etc., of agricultural Southern (poor) black field slaves. However, given the discriminatory effects of the society against them, they became, as the European Protestant whites were under Catholic feudalism, "unready-to-hand" seeking equality of opportunity, recognition, and distribution either in a national position of their own or via integration and assimilation.

Given these "unready-to-hand" response amongst the more free and powerful majority of the descendants of African slaves, who constituted the black bourgeoisie but were barred from reorganizing and reproducing their African institutions within the material resource framework of the American Protestant bifurcated social and economic order, it is in terms of the structural variables (class and status, given the economic basis for the social relations of the society) of the Protestant American society, not other factors, that black consciousnesses in America became, can be, and has been assessed and determined. Other practical consciousnesses amongst blacks within American society were defined and relationally delimited, present-at-hand, as "other" by whites and these blacks, the "best" of the house servants, mulattoes, artisans, and the educated free Negro from the North, who, when they became institutional regulators within the American social structure, delimited or represented, present-at-hand, the "proper" and "pure" way of being-in-the-world for all blacks in terms of Protestant liberal heterosexual bourgeois practical consciousness, interests, ideals, habitus, etc., against the language game and material conditions of the black poor in the Deep South who operated ready-to-hand, unready-to-hand, and present-at-hand within the systemicity of the Protestant Ethic and the spirit of capitalism.

Thus, "after the end of the [(slave)] trade in America in the latter half of the eighteenth and early part of the nineteenth centuries [Africanisms] importance as an explanation of slave personality declines: only about 400,000 native-born Africans had been brought to the United States before 1807 [(the slave trade, as sanctioned by the US Constitution, legally ended in 1808)]. Since an overwhelming percentage of nineteenth-century Southern slaves were native Americans" (Blassingame, 1972, pg., 39), they, about 3,953,760 of the black population at the outbreak of the Civil War, had to construct their identity or consciousness as a deployable unit of the American social structure in relation to and led by the social class language game of "the best of the house servants, who were freed by their masters, [and] the educated free Negro from the North" who together numbered about 500, 000, twelve percent of the total black population, "at the outbreak of the Civil War," against the social class language game of the black poor in agricultural slavery, and sought equality of opportunity, recognition, and distribution with their white counterparts[6] (See Table 6.1).

So it was not "in the process of acculturation the slaves made European forms serve African functions" (Blassingame, 1972: 17) as many scholars contend (Allen, 2001; Asante, 1988, 1990; Billingsley, 1968, 1970, 1993; Blassingame, 1972; Early, 1993; Gilroy, 1993; Gutman, 1976; Herskovits, 1958 [1941]; Holloway, 1990a; Karenga, 1993; Levine, 1977; Lewis, 1993; Lincoln and Mamiya, 1990; Nobles, 1987; Staples, 1978; Stack, 1974; West and Gates, 1997; West, 1993). On the contrary, the majority of slaves had to relationally define and choose, for their ontological security within the American social structure, between the European forms prescribed, present-at-hand, by power (whites and the best of the house servants, mulattoes, artisans, and the educated free Negro from the North) or the continual practice of their ontologically insecure "other" (African) forms of being-in-the-world or any "other" fully visible, albeit discriminated against, "alternatives," which delimited the social structure.

This does not mean that nothing of Africa survived slavery because of the African's need to forsake African forms in order to move from being "other" in American Protestant liberal bourgeois society. The suggestion here is that different alternative categorical boundaries or social class language groups existed, ready-to-hand, unready-to-hand, and present-at-hand, in the African community, and it was the "practical consciousness" of "the best of the house servants, mulattoes, artisans, and the educated free Negro from the North" that, to a large extent rejected African forms in order to be recognized by their white masters, which became dominant. Rejection of African forms would come to represent and define black identity/practical consciousness as these blacks became institutional regulators and the bearers of ideological and linguistic domination within the "class racism" of the dominant Protestant American society where they, unready-to-hand and present-at-hand, sought equality of opportunity, recognition, and distribution with their white counterparts against the material conditions and practices of the black poor in the Deep South (Reed, 1997; Winant, 2001).

Thus, in terms of the structural logic and differentiation presented here the idea is that in the development of American society within an emerging global economic colonial world-system, white, Protestant males developed, present-at-hand, a series of laws and judicial rulings, "enframed" (Heidegger's term) by the cultural metaphysical ideology of their protestant ethic, to define and represent the African (black cursed son of Ham, ungodly, licentious, emotional, undeveloped, irrational, uncivilized and barbaric, soul-less, etc.) situation in relation to whites (white, godly, pious, obedient, pure, civilized, diligent, rational, industrial, developed, etc.) within the class division and social relations of production of a Protestant global capitalism. Whites' morally justified (given the internal contradiction between slavery and Christian brotherhood, human rights, etc.) reproduced the integrative economic

Table 4.1. Growth of the Slave and Free Negro Population in the United States 1790–1860

CENSUS YEAR	NEGRO POPULATION			
	Total	Free Number	Free Per Cent	Slave
1860	4,441,830	488,070	11	3,953,760
1850	3,638,808	134,495	11.9	3,204,313
1840	2,873,648	386,293	13.4	2,487,355
1830	2,328,642	319,599	13.7	2,009,043
1820	1,771,656	233,634	13.2	1,538,022
1810	1,377,808	186,446	13.5	1,191,362
1800	1,002,037	108,435	10.8	893,602
1790	757,181	59,557	7.9	697,624

Note: Adapted From *The American Negro: His History and Literature* (p. 5), by E. Franklin Frazier, 1968, New York: Arno Press and The New York Times. Copyright 1968 by Arno Press, Inc.

(Protestant) social relations of agricultural production (slavery) proffered by them as the predestined or power elites of the society via ideology and ideological apparatuses to sustain their industrial developed base and bring about civilization to the black backward undeveloped "damned" African. As the historian Vincent D. Harding (1981) highlights,

> Beginning in Virginia at the end of the 1630s, laws establishing lifelong [(*durante vita*)] African slavery were instituted.[7] They were followed by laws prohibiting black-white intermarriage, laws against the ownership of property by Africans, laws denying blacks all basic political rights (limited as they were among whites at the time). In addition, there were laws against the education of Africans, laws against the assembling of Africans, laws against the ownership of weapons by Africans, laws perpetuating the slavery of their parents to African children, laws forbidding Africans to raise their hands against whites even in self-defense.
>
> Then, besides setting up legal barriers against the entry of black people as self-determining participants into the developing American society, the laws struck another cruel blow of a different kind: they outlawed many rituals connected with African religious practices [(which were deemed heathenistic, lewd, licentious, etc.)], including dancing and the use of the drums. In many places they also banned African languages. Thus they attempted to shut black people out from both cultures, to make them wholly dependent neuters.
>
> Finally, because the religious and legal systems were so closely intertwined, everywhere in the colonies a crucial legislative decision declared that the Africans' conversion to Christianity [(the Protestant type)] did not affect their enslavement . . . Again, Virginia led the way: in 1667 its Assembly passed an act declaring that "the conferring of baptism doth not alter the condition of the person as to his bondage or freedome." Such laws freed many whites to do their Christian duty of evangelization and to reap the profit and the social standing of slave ownership at the same time (27).

Africans who began arriving on the North American mainland "over more than a century preceding the War of Independence" (Gutman, 1976, pg., 328) did not initially subscribe to this racial, class, gendered, patriarchal ideological foundation. They resisted enslavement and its institutionalization through ship mutinies prior to their arrival to the "New World;" guerilla wars; rebellions, the New York City Revolt in 1712, the Stono, South Carolina revolt in 1739, Gabriel Prosser revolt in 1800, Denmark Vesey conspiracy in 1822, the Nat Turner revolt in 1831, etc.—over 250 revolts are recorded in the US; suicide and infanticide; flights; and sabotage, i.e., breaking tools and destroying crops, shamming illness or ignorance, taking property, spontaneous, and planned strikes, work slow-downs, self-mutilation, arson, attacks on whites and poisoning of slaveholders and their families (Karenga, 1993; Bennett, 1982; Harding, 1981; Blassingame, 1972; Gutman, 1976; Aptheker, 1964; Franklin and Moss, 2000). These efforts, however, proved to be counter productive to resisting subjugation, as they were incorporated, "present-at-hand," in the ideologies and ideological apparatuses of the white masters as evidence of the African's barbaric or savage disposition. The image of the African as unruly, rebellious, irrational, stupid, prone to thievery, destructive, sophomoric, licentious, were in turn used, relationally, to demonstrate to the slaves—during the "seasoning" process where the African learned Protestantism and its systematic work ethic—what was unacceptable behavior of a barbaric black slave without religion.

As the historian John Blassingame (1972) points out in *The Slave Community*, "white ministers taught the slaves that they did not deserve freedom, that it was God's will that they were enslaved, that the devil was creating those desires for liberty in their breasts, and that runaways would be expelled from the church. Then followed the slave beatitudes: blessed are the patient, blessed are the faithful, blessed are the cheerful, blessed are the submissive, blessed are the hardworking, and above all, blessed are the obedient" (Blassingame, 1972, pgs., 62-63).[8] During the "seasoning" process, where the newly arrived Africans were forcefully taught by slave masters, over-seers and native-born slaves the language, religion, and work ethic (purposive-rationality) of the Protestant American social structure. The majority of the early slaves, Stanley Elkins's (1959) Sambo, who worked intimately with their white masters, for their ontological security, incorporated, ready-to-hand, these beliefs and practices, which they recursively organized and reproduced in their own material practices, and they became the structural terms of "good moral character, Standard English, economic accumulation, temperance, industry, thrift, and learning," by which the larger slave community, which either maintained some element of their Africanisms in their material practices or developed a pathological-pathogenic form of the structural terms of the society given their relative isolation and poverty, was assessed, present-at-hand by the former, Sambos (Elkins, 1959; Frazier, 1939, 1957; Stampp, 1956; Genovese, 1974).

With their very survival dependent upon following rules of sanctioned conduct, many Africans accepted and acculturated or accommodated, ready-to-hand, to the institution of slavery and incorporated the Protestant ethos (its work ethic, family organization, "white standards of morality", godliness, obedience, rationalism, etc.), as defined, present-at-hand, by white and black agents of the Protestant Ethic and the spirit of capitalism, into their way of being-in-the-world or what amounted to the same thing the social structure (Elkins, 1959; Frazier, 1939, 1957; Stampp, 1956; Genovese, 1974). They and the dominant whites, as bearers of ideological and linguistic domination, used that Protestant socioreligious work ethos and the language game of their masters to assess and determine the proper rules of conduct for the larger slave community.[9] Those who did not accommodate were for the most part killed or brutally tortured until they complied. As a deployable unit, black slaves of the social structure, the social organization of family and cultural life in the majority of the African slave quarters became based on the ethical rules of the Protestant Ethic against fully visible African ways of being-in-the-world, as demonstrated in the practices of newly arrived Africans or those who, through the constitution of alternative meanings and behaviors through ego-centered communicative discourse, drives of the body, etc., either rejected the substantive and purposive-rationality of the American social structure or sought to exercise them in "a national position"[10] of their own. This latter group of blacks included maroone communities of runaway slaves who attempted to exercise their African agential moments in the new world order, and nationalist and conservative literate black leaders such as Booker T. Washington, David Walker, Gabriel Prosser, Denmark Vesey, Nat Turner, Martin Delany, Henry Highland Garnet, etc., who, although they embodied the Protestantism of the social structure, sought not integration, like the majority of their liberal bourgeois male counterparts, but separation and black nationalism (Meier, 1963, 1966; Stuckey, 1987).

Consequently, the agential moments of those blacks who failed to exercise the substantive and purposive-rationality of the society, or rejected it in order to exercise them in "a national position" of their own, were discriminated against and marginalized. Slave owners, white overseers, and native-born acculturated liberal blacks, "the best of the house servants, mulattoes, artisans, and the educated free Negro from the North," recursively organized and reproduced the purposive-rationality of the social structure, "the standard of good society," i.e., "Standard English, temperance, industry, thrift, and learning", in their own material practices, for the sole purpose of integration in order to obtain equality of opportunity, distribution, and recognition in the society with their white counterparts against the language and material conditions of the black poor and other groups, feminists, homosexuals, etc. (Meier and Rudwick, 1966 [1976], pg., 127).[11]

What developed from all this was a class-color-caste system, i.e. a "racial caste in class," superordinate industrial whites and subordinate agricultural blacks, perpetually subordinate, each dominated by the "predestined" class. Blacks in relation to whites, in other words, emerged in the social structure of the "spirit of colonial capitalism" as a caste (a racial class-in-itself as a result of "racial" structural differentiation) defined by their inherent fitness for slave agricultural labor to produce economic gain for their white masters, to a "caste in class" defined in relation to whites by those good obedient slaves (Stanley Elkins' Sambo, resulting from "class" structural differentiation), who embodied the language game and Protestant work ethic of the society for the sole purpose of integration or proving their predestination and those who did not because of their lack of "class" or need for separation.

This racial class social system became "reinforced" by the sociopolitical, religious, economic "legal system" (slavery and Jim Crow segregation) in which the majority of the Africans followed the rules of conduct which were sanctioned by the master for the slave and himself (Drake, 1965, pg. 3).[12] The majority of the slaves, given their "seasoning" in the American Protestant solidarity as a structurally differentiated racial class-in-itself, black slaves,[13] recursively reorganized and reproduced the rules and language of their masters, against the reproduced negative images (unruly, barbaric, savages, etc.) of themselves by these same masters. To demonstrate their "predestination", or a sense of self-worth, blacks acculturated European and Protestant practices within the social structure among themselves: speaking Standard English; jumping over the broomstick to legalize marriages, an old English tradition commonly used instead of church weddings, which were illegal for slaves; establishing traditional patriarchal nuclear families based on monogamy; establishing, as a result of segregation, Masonic lodges, churches, and mutual aid societies patterned after their white counterparts; demonstrating diligence in their work; instilling in their children a sense of Christian values;[14] black hymns; penning petitions for their liberation—the idea "that God granted temporal freedom, which man, without God's consent, had stolen away" (Blassingame,1972, pg. 63),—based on reason and revelation as their white masters did against England; and a developing class distinction (also based on color, lighter blacks v, darker ones) between house, "mixed-bloods," Negroes and field slaves, the former, given their close ties to the slave owner and quasi-freedom, better off then the latter (Franklin, 1957; Karenga, 1993; Bennett, 1982; Harding, 1981; Blassingame, 1972; Gutman, 1976; Aptheker, 1964; Franklin and Moss, 2000).[15]

This acculturation for survival in essence eventually turned African consciousness among a *few* blacks, "favored" slaves, house slaves, artisans, "mixed-bloods", free colored population, who together numbered about 500, 000 at the outbreak of the Civil War, into an American, black heterosexual liberal bourgeois Protestant type. A practical consciousness amongst many blacks defined (by black heterosexual men), unready-to-hand and present-at-hand, by their struggle for freedom, to exercise the purposive-rationality of the social structure and obtain class and status "based upon possession of money, education, and family background as reflected in distinctive styles of behavior" (Drake, 1965, pg. 3), against the claim of "their inherent fitness for slavery and backwardness" as highlighted amongst the language game of the black underclass, which delimited the social structure and barred them from achieving economic gain and recognition. This social psychological identity, represented most dynamically in the figure W.E.B. Du Bois and his double consciousness construct, stood in contradistinction to the social class language games of black heterosexual male conservatism, black nationalism, the ethos of black folk culture, and the material conditions and so-called pathologies, Black English Vernacular, emotionalism, promiscuity, poverty, single-headed households, etc., of the black underclass. In fact, heterosexual black male bourgeois Protestant liberalism would come to dominate as the dominant social psychological identity and player in the black quest for freedom, paradoxically, from the vagaries and contradictions of liberal bourgeois heterosexual white male Protestantism. Following the American Civil War and the black migrations from the rural agricultural South to the urban industrial North and Midwest, the nuclear family, the Protestant Ethic, Standard American English, education, and wealth, as defined, present-at-hand, by "favored" slaves, house slaves, artisans, "mixed-bloods", free colored population, who together numbered about 500, 000 at the outbreak of the Civil War constituted the practical consciousness of the black bourgeoisie and as a result the bearers of ideological and linguistic domination in black America against the purposive-rationality, female-headed households, promiscuity, Black/African American English Vernacular (BEV/AAEV), illiteracy, poverty, etc., of Southern agricultural blacks and the urban segregated black poor, whose bodies, language, practices, etc., were a result of racial-class divisions and social relations of agricultural and industrial production. The former sought, unready-to-hand and present-at-hand, equality of opportunity, recognition, and distribution for the latter. Double consciousness, hybridity, intersectionality, etc., represent their concepts, psychological pathologies, and practical consciousnesses amidst the continual discriminatory effects of the society.

BLACK AMERICA TODAY

Although, contemporarily, the postindustrial service occupations by which American capitalist society seeks economic gain, with its emphasis on consumerism and material wealth, conceal the Puritanical Protestantism that "enframes" or structure the society (albeit, contemporarily, material wealth as opposed to frugality is seen as a sign of God's grace, blessings, and salvation in the prosperity gospel that would emerge in neoliberal globalization). The purposive-rationality of the society's ideology and ideological apparatuses/institutions are still grounded in the mysticism of the Protestant ethic and spirit of capitalism through what Weber calls the ever-increasing, purposive, rationalization of the world. That is, the purposive-rational intent, through the contemporary process of (neoliberal) globalization, continues to be to integrate all peoples the world over into the class division and social relations of production of the Protestant mysticism, hard work, economic gain, etc., of the American nation which is presented in its educational apparatuses as the rational nature of the world as such, so as to obtain economic gain or capital accumulation and material wealth via agricultural, industrial, and postindustrial work as a sign of God's grace, blessings, and salvation.

Contemporarily, American blacks, as interpellated (workers) and embourgeoised agents of the American dominated global capitalist social structure of inequality, represent the most modern (i.e. socialized) people of color, in terms of their "practical consciousness," in this process of homogenizing social actors as agents of the protestant ethic or disciplined workers working for owners of production in order to obtain economic gain, status, and upward mobility in the larger American society (Frazier, 1957; Wilson, 1978; Glazer and Moynihan, 1963). Whereas, they once occupied the social space as agricultural and industrial workers, the former less educated than the latter, which were much wealthier because of their education and industrial work and therefore made education and industry the means to economic gain and upward economic mobility. Today, they continue to constitute the social space and their practical consciousness in terms of their relation to the means of production in post-industrial capitalist America, which differentiates black America for the most part into two status groups, a dwindling middle and upper class (living in suburbia) that numbers about 25 percent of their population (13 percent) and obtain their status as doctors, athletes, entertainers, lawyers, teachers, and other high-end professional service occupations; and a growing segregated "black underclass" of unemployed and under-employed wage-earners occupying poor inner-city communities and schools focused solely on technical skills, multicultural education, athletics, and test-taking for social promotion given the relocation of industrial and manufacturing jobs to poor periphery and semi-periphery countries and the introduction of low-end post-industrial service jobs and a growing informal economy in American urban-cities. Consequently, the poor performance of black American students, vis-à-vis whites, in education as an ideological apparatus for this post-industrial capitalist sociolinguistic worldview leaves them disproportionately in this growing underclass at the bottom of the American class social structure of inequality unable to either transform their world as they encounter it, or truly exercise their embourgeoisement given their lack of, what sociologist Pierre Bourdieu (1973, 1984) refers to as, capital (cultural, social, economic, and political).[16]

Ironically, contrary to John Ogbu's (1986) burden of acting white hypothesis, it is due to their indigent (pathological-pathogenic) class structural position within the American dominated global capitalist social structure of inequality, as opposed to a differing or oppositional cultural ethos from that of the latter, as to the reason why black American school children achieve and paradoxically underachieve vis-à-vis their white counterparts. The majority of black school children underachieve in school in general and on standardized test in particular, vis-à-vis their white counterparts, not because they possess or are taught (by their peers) at an early age distinct normative values from that of the dominant classes in the social structure that transfer into cultural and political conflict in the classroom as an ideological apparatus for capitalists. To the contrary, black students underachieve in school because in acquiring the "verbal behavior" of the dominant social structure in segregated "poor" gentrified inner-city communities which lack good legal industrial jobs and affordable resources that have been outsourced by capital to the Third World or developing countries, the majority, who happen to be less educated in the "Standard English" of the society, have reinforced a linguistic community or status group, the black underclass, financed by the upper-class of owners and high-level executives, as the bearers of ideological and linguistic domination for black America in particular and blacks all over the world in general (Mocombe, 2006, 2011; Mocombe and Tomlin, 2012).

That is, industrial work, which once dominated the American urban landscape, has disappeared or been outsourced to developing countries in favor of high finance postindustrial service work and an informal economy, which requires language skills and a level of education suitable to service consumers and investors. America's transition to a postindustrial, financialized service, economy beginning in the 1970s, decentered black bourgeois identity with its emphasis on economic gain, status, and upward mobility via the church and education, and reified and positioned black American underclass ideology and language, hip-hop culture and athletics, as a viable means for black American youth to achieve economic gain, status, and upward economic mobility in the society over education. Finance capital in the US beginning in the 1970s began investing in entertainment and other service industries where the inner-city language, entertainment and athletic culture of black (underclass) America became both a commodity and the means to economic gain for the black poor in America's postindustrial economy, which subsequently outsourced its industrial work to semi-periphery nations thereby blighting the inner-city communities. Blacks, many of whom migrated to the northern cities from the agricultural south looking for industrial work in the north following the Civil War (1861-1865), became concentrated in blighted communities where work began to disappear, schools were underfunded, and poverty increased. The black migrants, which migrated North with their BEV/AAEV from the agricultural South, became segregated sociolinguistic underclass communities, ghettoes, of unemployed laborers looking to illegal, athletic, and entertainment activities (running numbers, pimping, prostitution, drug dealing, robbing, participating in sports, music, etc.) for economic success, status, and upward mobility. Educated in the poorly funded schools of the urban ghettoes, given the process of deindustrialization and the flight of capital to the suburbs, with no work prospects, many black Americans became part of a permanent, (African American English Vernacular) AAEV speaking and poorly educated underclass looking to other activities for economic gain, status, and upward economic mobility. Those who were educated became a part of the social class language game of the Standard-English-speaking black middle class of professionals, i.e., teachers, doctors, lawyers, etc. (the black bourgeoisie), living in the suburbs, while the uneducated or poorly educated constituted the social class language game of the black underclass of the urban ghettoes. Beginning in the late 1980s, finance capital began commodifying and distributing (via the media industrial complex) the social class language game of the underclass black culture for entertainment in the emerging postindustrial economy of the US over the ideology and language, social class language game, of the black bourgeoisie. Be that as it may, efforts to succeed academically among black Americans, which constituted the ideology and language of the black bourgeoisie, paled in comparison to their efforts to succeed as speakers of Black English, athletes, "gangstas", "playas", and entertainers, which became the ideology and language of the black underclass living in the inner-cities of America. Authentic black American identity became synonymous with black underclass hip-hop ideology and language.

Hence, contemporarily, black American students have a peer status group in the American dominated global capitalist social structure of inequality with its own language, style of dress, music, etc. Contemporarily, the group is institutionalized or occupies a status position in the American postindustrial class social structure of inequality based for the most part on their academic (under) achievement and social relation to the means of production, and not their race. The poor academic achievement of black American students, which initially results from their "linguistic structure," disproportionately leaves them at the bottom of the educational system, which leads to poor or no jobs in the American post-industrial labor market, which has transferred its industrial jobs overseas for higher paying financial jobs. As such, the status group is constituted as a class of poorly educated and unemployed or poorly employed laborers, living in predominantly inner-cities where low technical work has disappeared for low paying service and higher paying financial jobs. They, the black underclass, are unable to achieve a better life chance compared to those well educated and employed in high paying service occupations and therefore turn to other activities (drug dealing, sports, hustling, music, etc.) in the formal and informal economy that are more likely to payoff in the society given their poor linguistic skills and education, and the outsource of industrial jobs overseas by capital.

Subsequently, the material conditions and practices of this black underclass social psychologically have given rise to celebrated ideological and linguistic structures (Hip-Hop culture and Black/African-American English Vernacular), which appear to stand in contradistinction to the ideology and language (Standard English) of middle class black bourgeois and white America. This "mismatch of linguistic social class function" as constituted through and by the commodification of hip-hop culture is an appearance because the practical consciousness of this black underclass is no different from middle and upper middle class black folks. Their purposive-rational end within the class division and social relations of production of American capitalism remains economic gain, status, and upward mobility in the society just like that of middle and upper middle class black folks. Only the ideological apparatuses by which they are interpellated and embourgeoised and the means to those ends, economic gain, status, and upward mobility, have changed in a jobless post-industrial American material condition: poor schools, the streets, and prisons became the dominant ideological apparatuses by which they are interpellated and embourgeoised; and athletics, music, entertaining, hustling, etc. serve as means to achieving economic gain, status, and upward mobility over the educational avenues paved by the social class language game of the black and white middle and upper class suburban America. That is, given the commodification by finance capital of black American underclass practices as hip-hop culture and the predominance of the entertainment industry, media, etc., as the medium for its mass dissemination in the American post-industrial landscape, presently, they, the black American underclass of poorly educated and poorly (un) employed laborers, have become the bearers of ideological and linguistic domination in black America to the chagrin of their working, middle, and upper-middle class brethrens living in the suburbs and obtaining economic gain from their education based professions. Many black students growing up in inner-cities around the world no longer identify with academic achievement and success as means to obtaining economic gain as previously outlined by the social class language game of the black middle and upper classes, but instead they identify with the material practices of the black American underclass, which is over-represented and glorified in the media through hip-hop and athletic cultures, and seek to have their "blackness" as defined by that status group pay-off for them at the expense of achieving academically as defined by the black professional class working in high-end service occupations.

This is the social structural and social psychological manifestation of the burden of acting white hypothesis within an American dominated post-industrial capitalist social structure of inequality that predominantly differentiates along class lines, and has institutionalized Black English, athletics, the entertainment industry, hustling, etc., financed by capital, as viable means or social functional roles to economic gain, status, and upward mobility in the larger American society for black America over more academically oriented careers. It is this economic payoff associated with hustling, sports, entertainment, etc., for underachieving blacks in the larger American society, which perpetuates the achievement gap, and prevents all effective corrective measures implemented by school systems from achieving complete success to reorient black functional roles in the society to more academically oriented careers (Mocombe, 2001, 2006, 2011; Mocombe and Tomlin, 2010).

As black youth become adolescents they are disadvantaged in school by the social functions the black American underclass and the larger mainstream society reinforces. That is, success or economic gain amongst the "black underclass," who speak or adopt Black/African American English Vernacular, listen to hip-hop music, participate in sports, is not measured by status obtained through education as in the case of black bourgeois middle class standards; on the contrary, athletics, music, and other activities (illegal ones) not typically "associated" with educational attainment, but which they are rewarded for by finance capital if they work hard, etc., serve as the means to success or economic gain, status, and upward mobility. Thus effort in school, in terms of academics, in general suffers, and as a result test scores and grades are further impacted. That is, for these youth, especially the black male in the society, there is no logical and obvious connection between academics and economics in their poor and blighted cities; instead, sports, music, drugs, etc., appear to be more accessible and viable means for improving their life goal of economic gain as opposed to the education promulgated by the "black bourgeoisie," which has expanded, contemporarily, to include athletes, rap-stars, hustlers, and other black entertainers (Frazier, 1957). This has led to a retention and expulsion rate in black America for example that is doubled that of whites, 33 and 18 percent respectively; an ever-increasing criminalization of black urban America, 43.9 percent of the state and federal prison populations; the ever-increasing proletarianization of the black masses; and an ever-increasing academic achievement gap that has the black bourgeois professional class clamoring that there is a conspiracy in the capitalist social system to destroy black boys.

It is this "mismatch of linguistic social class function," the ideals of middle class black bourgeois (standardized) America against the so-called "pathologies" (functions) of the black underclass, Ogbu and other post-segregationist black middle-class scholars inappropriately label, "acting-white" or culture of poverty.

The black underclass in America's ghettoes has slowly become, since the 1980s, replacing their middle-class brethrens in suburbia, the bearers of ideological and linguistic domination for the black community in America and the world over. Their language (Ebonics or Black English Vernacular) and worldview as commodified through hip hop culture and financed by capital have become the means by which black youth (and youth throughout the world) attempt to recursively organize and reproduce their material resource framework against the means or social roles of black bourgeois middle class America. The aim, in an American post-industrial landscape that has commodified black hip-hop and athletic culture as means to economic gain, status, and upward economic mobility is no longer to seek status and economic gain through a Protestant Ethic that stresses hard work, diligence, differed gratification, and education; on the contrary, sports, music, instant gratification, illegal activities (drug dealing), and skimming are the dominant means portrayed.

Schools, with their emphasis in the postindustrial society on celebrating diversity, throughout urban inner cities are no longer means to a professional end in order to obtain economic gain, status, and upward mobility, but obstacles to that end. That is, schools in urban American centers are no longer means to achieving economic success, status, or prestige in the society for young blacks, males in particular; instead, the focus on cooperative group works, cultural sensitivity training, and dialogical processes become the acculturative means of training blacks on how to market their underclass linguistic community and social roles as athletes and entertainers to others in both the American postindustrial economy and the global marketplace under American hegemony (Mocombe, 2007). Hence black youth are not "acting white" when education no longer becomes a priority or the means to economic status as they get older; they are attempting to be white and achieve bourgeois economic status in the society by being "black" in a racialized post-industrial capitalist social structure wherein the economic status of "blackness" is (over) determined by white capitalists and the black proletariats of the West, the black underclass, whose way of life, language, and image ("athletes and hip-hopsters") has been commodified (by white and black capitalists) and distributed throughout the world (via the black entertainment television network BET) for entertainment, (black) status, and economic purposes. Paul Gilroy's and Cornel West's, "present-at-hand," usurpation of Du Boisian double consciousness to define black bourgeois consciousness in relation to the material conditions of the urban black underclass ideologically attempts to do for this shift in the social relations of production, from agricultural to industrial to post-industrial, what Du Bois attempted to do in defining black bourgeois consciousness in relation to the material conditions of blacks in the agricultural deep south following the end of the Civil War. Just the same, the theory of intersectionality among black bourgeois academics highlight the discourse by which variant subjective positions have been marginalized and prevented from achieving equality of opportunity, recognition, and distribution within the global (postindustrial) capitalist social structure of class inequality and differentiation of the US, UK, and the diaspora. Be that as it may, by no means can double consciousness and intersectionality be viewed, against the discourse of the pathological-pathogenic, adaptive-vitality, anti-essentialist, and anti-anti-essentialist positions, as the universal mechanism by which black consciousness and communities were constituted as their rhetoric, like black consciousness and black communities in the US, UK, and the diaspora are the unready-to-hand and present-at-hand by-product (bourgeois ideology) of the global (industrial and postindustrial) capitalist social structure of class inequality and differentiation, which attempts to structure the practices of subjective experiences within class differentiation and thereby control diversity and meaning constitution for capital accumulation. So it is within the racial class division and social relations of production that black American identity, and black diasporic identity must be understood. Contemporarily, the two dominant social class language games of black America are heavily influencing the diaspora via the material wealth of black preachers, educators, athletes, and entertainers.

NOTES

1. See Philip D. Curtin, *The Atlantic Slave Trade: A Census* (Madison, 1969), Pp.72-87.
2. See William Julius Wilson's *The Declining Significance of Race: Blacks and Changing American Institutions* (1978) for the economic and political dynamics involved in shaping Southern institutions.
3. Whether on large plantations or small ones, all enslaved Africans in interaction with whites developed their practical consciousness by warring against the ways of the slave master and what they said the slaves were based on the fully visible behavior of newly arrived Africans.
4. In our structural understanding, the origins of American slavery, and its relation to the ideology of racism, are social structural. Slavery in America was not an autonomous system which developed out "of the condition and status of seventeenth-century labor" (Elkins, 1968 [1972]), but, as Oscar and Mary F. Handlin imply (albeit for the Handlins their position was also in reference to economic conditions whereas we are taking their reference to encompass a structuring ontology that gives rise to institutions), slavery "emerged rather from the adjustment to American conditions of traditional European institutions" (Handlins, 1950 [1972], pg. 23), which gave rise to the necessary conditions for the ever-increasing need for cheaper laborpower, which was in-turn rationalized or justified within the order of things, i.e., the Protestant ethic and the spirit of capitalism.
5. See Joseph E. Holloway, "The Origins of African-American Culture," in Africanisms in American Culture (1990). Bloomington and Indianapolis: Indiana University Press, Pp. 2.
6. See E. Franklin Frazier's *Black Bourgeoisie* (1957), Pp. 15.
7. Massachusetts, founded by the Pilgrims, a Protestant sect, became the first colony (1641) to pass any enslavement laws.
8. It is no surprise that the seven major historic black denominations—the African Methodist Episcopal (A.M.E.) Church; the African Methodist Episcopal Zion (A.M.E.Z.) Church; the Christian Methodist Episcopal (C.M.E.) Church; the National Baptist Convention, U.S.A., Incorporated (NBC); the National Baptist Convention of America, Unincorporated (NBCA); the Progressive National Baptist Convention (PNBC); and the Church of God in Christ (COGIC)—that account for more than 80 percent of black religious affiliation in the United States are of the Baptist, Methodist, and Pentecostal Protestant variety. These Protestant churches with their high emotionalism, fervor, enthusiasm, and excitement, their revivalism, their excesses of sinning and high-voltage confessing (Bell, 1960: 103), have provided—for an illiterate mass prevented for a long time, on account of their immorality, lasciviousness, and heathenism, from partaking in the "thisworldly" affairs of the Protestant American social structure, derived from the intellectualism of traditional Protestantism—the means for access, via what is required for "otherworldly" existence, into the "thisworldly" affairs of the social structure.

In other words, for blacks, the Christianity of Methodism and Baptism served as a means to the Protestant ethic and the spirit of capitalism, the structuring structure of the culture that is American society. The "Christianity that was spread among slaves during the First and Second Awakenings was an evangelical Christianity that stressed personal conversion through a deep regenerating experience, being born again. The spiritual journey began with an acknowledgement of personal sinfulness and unworthiness and ended in an emotional experience of salvation by God through the Holy Spirit. The rebirth meant a change, a fundamental reorientation in the approach to life" (Lincoln and Mamiya, 1990: 6)—becoming moral agents of the Protestant ethic in "this world" in order to have access to the "other world."
9. Some historians argue that the period prior to the cessation of the slave trade was more brutal and harsh than the period after the ban when slave masters relied almost completely on natural increase to reproduce the labor force. In our view, this distinction underestimates the degree to which the enslaved blacks' ontological security (the degree of brutality and oppres-

siveness) was attached to following plantation rules of conduct. In essence, our position is whether benign or brutal the general intent of the institution of slavery, as an ideological institution, was to inhibit the general autonomy and determine the agential moments of blacks. Just like the general intent of the organization of work in contemporary times is to maintain the capitalist social relations of production and determine the agential moments of all wage laborers.

10. Martin Robinson Delany quoted in August Meier and Elliott Rudwick, *From Plantation to Ghetto* (New York, 1976), Pp. 151.

11. As August Meier and Elliott Rudwick (1966 [1976]) point out, this was the platform of the "Negro Convention Movement," which began in 1830 and met annually until the end of the century. A predominantly Northern phenomenon, "led and attended by the most distinguished leaders of the race—prominent ministers, physicians, lawyers, businessmen, and, after the Civil War, politicians . . . the conventions provide illuminating insight into the thinking of articulate blacks on the problems facing the race" such as slavery and the discrimination and "indignities" of the free colored folks (126).

12. To practice their traditional African ways would bring about cruel and unusual punishments, even death, considering that the African was, for the most part, under twenty-four hour surveillance in order to prevent insurrections. There is a debate amongst historians of slavery, who argue over the extent to which blacks within slavery had some form of autonomy. As can logically be deduced, the historians of the adaptive-vitality school (Blassingame, Gutman, Franklin, etc.) maintain that blacks were able to retain some of their African cultural heritage because they were to some extent autonomous. The historians of the pathological-pathogenic school (Elkins, Stampp, Genovese, etc.) argue to the contrary.

13. It should be noted that a debate lingers regarding the origins of African spirituality. Given that the Africans were prevented from establishing any institutions to reproduce their ethos in the colonies, we rather agree with E. Franklin Frazier's (1957) understanding:

> The most important institution which the Negro has built in the United States is the Negro church. Contrary to the claim of some students of the Negro that the Negro church was an African survival resurrected on American soil, the Negro church is a product of the American environment. The form of its organization and the character of its religious services were the result of the proselyting of Protestant missionaries, especially the Baptist and the Methodist missionaries. This does not mean that the Negro's peculiar experience in America did not contribute to the shaping of the institution. The influence of the Negro's experience in the building of his church is seen in the variations in the character of the Negro church, which reflect the extent of the Negro's education and isolation in American life and his economic and social status (87).

14. The character of the black family during slavery was so patterned after the institutional regulators of the American social structure that today there is talk of its disintegration resulting not from slavery, as E. Franklin Frazier (1939) proclaimed, but from the post-World War II public policies of welfare and job relocations out of urban, which has fostered female-headed households, teenage pregnancy, promiscuity, welfare dependency, out-of-wedlock births, etc. See William Julius Wilson's (1987) *The Truly Disadvantaged* and Herbert Gutman's (1976) *The Black Family in Slavery and Freedom*.

15. "As long as the slaves communed with whites [(and remained illiterate)], their religious instruction was circumscribed. The planters, in spite of their piety, insisted that their slaves not learn any of the potentially subversive tenets [(which whites themselves had used against their former masters, the English crown)] of Christianity (the brotherhood of all men, for instance)" (Blassingame, 1972: 61). Once the slaves learned these tenets, their quest for freedom became a fight for their "God" given rights.

16. Pierre Bourdieu's (1984) theory of social reproduction refers to several forms of "capital" (cultural, economic, symbolic, and social). we will not go into details about Bourdieu's social reproduction theory, what we will say, however, is that the "capital" references refer to the institutional norms, resources, connections, etc. that one needs in their respective societies'

to participate in its cultural, economic, symbolic, and social life. Bourdieu posits that the possession of, for the most part, middle class "capital" is assumed by the educational system in contemporary society, but is not taught. Thus, education theorists (i.e., James Coleman), who have operationalized Bourdieu's concept, conclude, poor students enter school at a disadvantage (i.e., they lack "middle class capital), which leads to their "poor" achievement. The solution from this perspective is to teach and orient these poor students to more middle class values and norms so that they can achieve like their white counterparts. In the postindustrial economies of the US and UK, where the lack of capital is commodified and celebrated for capital accumulation, Bourdieu's theory is problematic in that to speak of the lack of capital, social, cultural, political, etc. as a barrier to upward economic mobility and status in the societies is no longer the case, and politically incorrect. Hence this need to develop a cultural realm to explain agency within capitalist relations of production as Bourdieu has done with his theory of praxis negates the agential moments of the actors through the commodification of their structural position, which brings Bourdieu's theory and the actions of those who lack capital back to the structural realm of analysis. This is why we refrain from using Bourdieu's cultural notions to outline the constitution of black American practical consciousness.

Chapter Five

Conclusions

The Constitution of African and Caribbean Life within the Protestant Ethic and the Spirit of Capitalism

Just as in the case of black Americans, race and class distinctions within black communities in Africa and the Caribbean must be understood as being constituted within and by the two dominant social class language games, a black bourgeoisie and underclass, created by the class division and social relations of production of global capitalism or the capitalist world-system during slavery, colonialism, decolonization, and the present (neoliberal) globalization era under American hegemony. Contemporarily, these two classes in Africa and the Caribbean are heavily influenced by the material influence of these two classes as they are constituted in black America via the amalgamated (black American and diasporic) criminal, hip-hop, and athletic and entertainment practical consciousness of the black American underclass; and the Protestant Ethic and spirit of capitalism of black preachers and educated professionals of the black American bourgeoisie. Via the nation-state building and globalizing processes highlighted in chapter three, their immigration patterns, and ideological apparatuses such as the black church, education, the streets, and the US media industrial complex Africa and the black diaspora is ever-so slowly becoming African-Americanized within the amalgamated racial-class structure of black America.

POST-EMANCIPATION PERIOD

Just as in the case of the black American, the blacks in Africa and the Caribbean were constituted as a racial-caste-in-class in the class division of the aforementioned global Protestant social relations of production in their home countries during slavery, colonialism, decolonization, and globalization. Within the racial-class division of the global Protestant social relations of production, i.e., world-system, what emerged among blacks in the Caribbean and Africa under slavery, colonialism, decolonization, and globalization was a twofold class system or social class language games, a black administrative bourgeoisie and a black (rural and urban) underclass (from which the working classes would be drawn), which discriminated against practical consciousnesses arrived at through the deferment of meaning in ego-centered communicative action; the drives of the body; and impulses of subatomic particles. In the Caribbean, the social class language game of the black underclass would be defined by its linguistic structure, patois, and class position/material conditions within the agricultural slavery of the islands, which stood against the social class language game—the education, embourgeoisement, and linguistic structure of the handful of men of color who ruled with the white power elites and adopted their language and class positions into their being-in-the-world—of the black (administrative) bourgeoisie of slavery and colonialism, and the working class who (as a result of their interpellation and embourgeoisement via the family, church, poor schools, and work) shared in the ideas and ideals of the latter. The same held true in Africa. In Africa the social class language game of the black underclass would be defined by its linguistic structure, the native language and practices of the different tribes of the continent, and their class position within the agricultural slavery of the continent, which stood against the social class language game of the African black (administrative) bourgeoisie and the working classes they interpellated and embourgeoised via their language, modes of production, ideologies, ideological apparatuses, and communicative discourse as prescribed by whites.

During the nation-state building era of the twentieth century in both the Caribbean and Africa, the black (administrative) bourgeoisie and their social class language game under the leadership and directorship of their former white (colonial) slavemasters would assume positions of power following slavery and decolonization against the working and underclass practical consciousness of their countrymen who they would attempt to interpellate and embourgeois with the language, mode of production, ideology, ideological apparatuses, and communicative discourse of the West. Albeit the glaring difference between Africa and the rest of the black diaspora, outside of Haiti, was that the African black bourgeoisie encountered a culturally distinct group whose material conditions were determined by their African form of system and social integration. In the rest of the Caribbean, outside of Haiti which paralleled Africa, the black bourgeoisie encountered a structurally differentiated black working and underclass in the cities and rural communities who shared (due to the ideological apparatuses, i.e., patriarchal family, church, and schools) in the ideology of the bourgeoisie in their poor material conditions (Klak, 1998; Mocombe, 2016).

Following decolonization and amidst the emerging neoliberal globalization era, many of the Caribbean islands remained in a state of economic bondage and political and social limbo in the development phase of the post-emancipation period (Lowenthal, 1972; Klak, 1998). Following slavery, plantation owners and governments throughout the Caribbean curtailed the freedom of laborers binding them to the estate so as to increase sugar production for the global marketplace while seeking to industrially develop their capital cities along the lines of Europe and America. During this industrial process of the development phase of the post-emancipation period, whites still owned the best lands. Unlike the black American experience, however, whites were less successful in preventing non-whites from acquiring land and producing crops such as cotton, coconuts, coffee, cacao, and bananas which replaced sugar, for export to the Metropoles. Generally, the black majority were forced to work for low wages or face hunger, eviction, or imprisonment. In places such as Suriname, the Windward Islands, Montserrat and the Virgin Islands, former slaves, like their African American counterparts, worked as sharecroppers. To add to the black/white racial dichotomy found throughout the islands, Chinese and Mandarin indentured laborers were introduced to the Caribbean economies to ensure both that wages were kept down and a steady labor supply for agribusinesses. As time progressed, these laborers entered the wholesale and retail trades and became peddlers. East Indians and Javanese workers were subsequently imported to work on the land. Indian indentured laborers endured harsh conditions and as the East Indian population increased in islands such as Trinidad, blacks, for the most part, moved off the sugar estates into the towns or small holdings to assume industrial (manufacturing) and service (tourism) work outsourced from First World (core) countries like the United States (US) and United Kingdom (UK). Hence, throughout the Caribbean what developed from this process of decolonization, nation-state building, industrialization, deagriculturalization, and urbanization of blacks was a socioeconomic system or social structure in which Chinese and Mandarin workers worked wholesale and retail trades; East Indians and Javanese workers occupied the agricultural sector; and blacks moved to the towns and cities to assume the administrative, industrial, and tourist and service duties left behind by many whites who left the islands following the post-emancipation period where the international community under the hegemony of the United States, England, and France dictated their economic roles in the global (Protestant) capitalist world-system (Klak, 1998; McMichael, 2008).

Hence in the contemporary global Protestant capitalist world-system under American hegemony, the majority of the Caribbean nations are periphery states where tourism, agribusiness, light manufacturing, and the athletic and entertainment industries constitute the modes of production prescribed to the black administrative bourgeoisie by the international community, IMF, World Bank, etc., under US and European hegemony for their citizenry (Klak, 1998). The black administrative bourgeoisie in-turn interpellate and embourgeois their citizenry via the language of their former colonial slavemasters, aforementioned modes of production, ideology (neoliberalism), ideological apparatuses (poor schools, prisons, streets of the urban slums, laws, police forces, etc.), and communicative discourse (economic gain, status, and upward mobility) of the West. These processes produced and produce two dominant social class language games, the black administrative bourgeoisie (educated bourgeois professionals, managers, and entrepreneurs) of the capital cities and underclass of rural communities and urban slums, fighting as the bearers of ideological and linguistic domination for the masses of unemployed and working classes of their citizenry.

Administratively, following decolonization, most ex-slaves participated in local affairs only marginally more than East Indians. In the French and British Caribbean, for instance, whites controlled the local legislature with a handful of men of color who were interpellated and embourgeoised, via the family, church, and schools, as middle class administrators, managers, and professionals of the colonial system. The twentieth and twenty-first centuries witnessed a shift in the power in the Caribbean, however. Following slavery and decolonization, blacks and other people of color increased their influence in government and other institutions under the middle class or European influences (embourgeoisement) of the handful of men of color who once ruled with whites. Although, the relationship between blacks and whites changed, the continued separation of the black majority from the white and brown minorities meant the poor, who were mainly blacks working in agricultural production for the global capitalist world-system, developed their own underclass patterns of behaviors and linguistic systems (patois), social class language game, based on rural and street life and activities, which became juxtaposed against the social class language game of the middle class and European identities of those in power, the handful of men of color who once ruled with whites and adopted their linguistic system, family structure, and class identity against the social class language game of the black poor (cf Alleyne, 1988). This color and class distinctions between whites, browns, and blacks still persist in the Caribbean in the twenty-first century. Despite the fact that blacks from the underclasses, given their interpellation and embourgeoisement via the patriarchal family, church, and education have gained significant positions of leadership, high status posts not held by whites remain a light-colored and middle class domain; however, this tendency has become less prominent since the independence of most Caribbean islands. Non-whites who are educated, have a middle class sensibility, and adopt the social class language games of the black administrative bourgeoisie, are in the majority in all government areas and occupy most places of public eminence, a development which has had a significant impact on public attitudes and class identities of those immigrating from the Caribbean to countries like the US, UK, etc.

Rural communities and the urban slums, contrarily, are constituted by those (working classes of the black underclass) employed in agribusinesses, light manufacturing, wholesale and retail trades, and the tourist industries. Those unable to seek employment in agribusinesses, light manufacturing, wholesale and retail trades, or tourism (the dominant modes of production in the Caribbean as prescribed by international institutions to the black administrative bourgeoisie) migrate to either the former Metropole and the US or the capital cities of their respective countries where they constitute a black working and underclass of unemployed and underemployed laborers looking to the streets, their musical genres, athletics, and cultural accoutrements (patois and food) from the rural areas and urban slums to achieve economic gain, status, and upward mobility. The working classes, interpellated by the family, church, and poorly funded schools, pattern their lifestyles after the black administrative bourgeoisie (who no longer pattern their lifestyles after whites, but successful images of blacks who are dominated by black Americans); and those unable to work pattern their lifestyles after the black underclasses of their home countries and America and seek to achieve economic gain, status, and upward mobility by hustling, criminal activities, athletics, or the entertainment industry.

These same class processes held and hold true for class and race relations on the African continent. The most glaring difference between the two social class language games that would emerge on the African continent and the Caribbean islands, however, is that the social class language game of the black underclass on the continent, like in Haiti, was able to maintain many of their traditional African linguistic systems and cultural practices, which became marginalized and discriminated against by the social class language game of the embourgeoised blacks who ruled with whites on the continent through ideological apparatuses such as the family, church, education, etc., and the social relations of production. Conversely, in the Caribbean, African culture among the black underclass and working classes were almost completely loss given their forced integration by whites into their racial-class divisions and the social relations of agricultural production. The divergences in Caribbean life between the practical consciousness of the black underclass and the black bourgeoisie are a result of their interpellation and embourgeoisement via different ideological apparatuses of the Protestant capitalist world-system: the patriarchal family, church, and schools in terms of the latter, the black bourgeoisie; poorly-funded schools, the streets, and prisons in terms of the former, the black underclass. Nonetheless, as in the Caribbean, following decolonization the racial-class system in Africa would be reproduced via the patriarchal family, church, state, education, class division, and the social relations of production under the control of the social class language game of the embourgeoised handful of men of color (black administrative bourgeoisie) who once ruled with whites. The embourgeoised handful of men of color who once ruled with whites would serve as an administrative bourgeoisie for the global capitalist relations of production under the leadership of the upper-class of white owners and high-level executives operating in core nations such as the US, UK, France, etc., following decolonization. It would be through education (along with the family and churches, which remain in the hands of private individuals), as an ideological state apparatus under the directorship of the handful of men of color who once ruled with whites, that their social class language game and the class division and social relations of production of global capitalism would be organized and reproduced on the African continent and the Caribbean over the social class language game of the black underclass (who are predominantly interpellated and embourgeoised by the streets of the urban slums, prisons, and poorly funded schools). Both social class language games, the black bourgeoisie and the underclass, discriminated/discriminate against alternative practical consciousnesses, homosexuality, feminism, transgender, etc., arrived-at through the deferment of meaning in ego-centered communicative actions; the drives of the body; and impulses of subatomic particles. Albeit this trend of discriminating against alternative practical consciousnesses, homosexuality, feminism, transgender, etc., arrived-at through the deferment of meaning in ego-centered communicative actions, etc., in the black "Third" world is encountering several obstacles as the postindustrial First World because of their shift in production and ideological structure, which fosters identity politics for capital accumulation, is forcing the black diaspora to adopt the ideology of multiculturalism, identity politics, individual freedom, and human rights through transnational ideological apparatuses such as the UN, World Bank, IMF, etc. in their agricultural, industrial, and tourist economies whose ideological apparatuses, the family, church, education, etc., resembled the First World during the early phases of their Protestant capitalist development.

Contemporarily, education in the Caribbean and Africa, for the most part continues to be an elite privilege. The poor constitute a poorly educated/uneducated working/underclass (predominantly interpellated and embourgeoised by the patriarchal family, church, poorly funded rural and urban schools, prisons, and the streets of their urban slums), living either in the overcrowded Caribbean and African capital cities or small farm towns, looking to immigrate to the homeland (Metropoles) of their former colonial masters or the United States for work and better economic opportunities. The well-to-do, for the most part, pay for private, parochial education; upon completion, they subsequently send their children abroad for secondary schooling. In many instances, they either return back to the islands and the African continent where they assume administrative and bureaucratic roles in government or the private sector, or come to constitute a black bourgeois and working class of the Metropoles. Hence Caribbean and African societies, as well as its immigration pattern overseas, would become juxtaposed between, or against, a poorly educated/uneducated underclass of poor urban dwellers and former agricultural workers (predominantly interpellated and embourgeoised in the global Protestant capitalist world-system via their work, or lack thereof, the family, church, streets, poorly funded schools, and prisons), and an embourgeoised middle class of non-white administrators (predominantly interpellated through the patriarchal family, church, and prestigious schools at home and abroad) who, contemporarily, serve the same purpose as the handful of colored persons who administered the islands and the continent with whites during the colonial period. Both groups contemporarily in the age of globalization (1950s- to the present) under American hegemony are linguistically and ideologically heavily influenced through the media and the black church by the black American underclass and bourgeoisie.

In the class division and social relations of production of global Protestant capitalism, Caribbean and African societies, as well as their immigration pattern overseas, would become constituted by this poorly educated/uneducated working/underclass of criminals, hustlers, athletes, entertainers, agricultural, factory, and tourist workers/non-workers; and the embourgeoised middle class of non-white administrators who, contemporarily, serve the same purpose as the handful of colored persons who administered the islands and the continent with whites during the colonial period. It would be their (poorly educated underclass and the embourgeoised middle class of non-white administrators) historical experiences of immigration, unemployment, housing segregation, and industrialization and suburbanization within the world and America's Protestant capitalist social structure of class inequality that would subsequently lead to the constitution of black communities in the United States (US) and United Kingdom (UK) as a racial-caste-in-class interpellated, embourgeoised, and heavily influenced by the amalgamated language and ideology of the black American underclass and bourgeoisie.

Just as in the "great migration" of black Americans from the agricultural South to the industrial North where they became concentrated in urban inner-city environments, the immigration patterns of Caribbean and African blacks seeking work in America would lead them to settle in poor working and underclass urban inner-city environments, where work had disappeared to the suburbs and developing countries, populated by the black American underclass, which was becoming ever-increasingly divided from a black bourgeoisie that had relocated to the suburbs (Wilson, 1978; 1998). These black Caribbean and African immigrants already differentiated by class in their home countries would come to be interpellated and classified as blacks within the racial-class typology of American society. As such their experiences would come to be tied to the experiences of native black Americans even though in many instances they despised and disparaged black underclass practical consciousness, i.e., criminality, hip-hop and athletic culture. This meant that, on the one hand, the adults sought to become bourgeois and better themselves through education, work, and adopting the linguistic structure and ideology of their native and black American bourgeoisie as encapsulated in the prosperity gospel of the black church as influenced by megachurch preachers and entertainers in the likes of TD Jakes, Creflo Dollar, Eddie Long, Donnie McClurkin, Kim Burrell, etc., and educated black professionals. On the other hand, many of their children would come to fall into and influence (as black American underclass practical consciousness became an amalgamation of black diasporic practical consciousness) the practical consciousness and linguistic structure of the black underclass urban youth culture with its emphasis on Black English, athletics, entertainment, hip-hop culture, hustling, etc., as viable means to economic gain, status, and upward social mobility. As such, by the second generation, no differences would come to exist between the original African Americans and those from Africa and the Caribbean who would come to integrate and constitute the black bourgeoisie and underclass in America. Akon, Patrick Ewing, Dikembe Mutumbo, Jason Pierre-Paul, Mario Elie, Andre Drummond, Rihanna, Wyclef Jean, Biggie Smalls, etc. although from the Caribbean and Africa, they influenced (rap music would emerge as a cross between Jamaican musical genres and black American/Haitian blues, jazz, etc.), adopted, integrated, and constituted black underclass criminal, athletic, and entertainment practical consciousness, and their wealth catapulted them to the status positions of the black bourgeoisie, which they now export, in an amalgamated form, back to the black diaspora via the media industrial complex and their charitable works. Conversely, the parents, although residing in inner-cities that would come to constitute an ethnic immigrant community, which paralleled the Italian, Polish, Irish, and Jewish immigrant communities of the nineteenth century, would be interpellated and embourgeoised via the family structure, church, and education by the amalgamated black bourgeois class of America, which would influence the leadership, i.e., immigrant pastors, educated professionals, and entrepreneurs, of their ethnic black communities.

As such, whereas in their home countries their African-Americanization takes and took place through schools, the family and church, where Caribbean and African preachers, i.e., the late Dr. Myles Munroe, Bishop Noel Jones, Bishop David Oyedepo, Christian Oyakhilome, Temitope B. Joshua, Matthew Ashimolowo, etc., are heavily influenced by black American educated professionals, preachers, and entertainers in the likes of TD Jakes, Creflo Dollar, Juanita Bynum, Eddie Long, Bishop Jamal Bryant, Kim Burrell, etc. through their evangelism and televangelisms, on the one hand; and the hip-hop, athletic, and entertainment culture of black urban America which (in its African American manifestation, which conceals its diasporic elements) influences the black youth through their over-representation in the global media, on the other. In America, it is their immigration patterns coupled with racial-class segregation which ties them to black America, and leads to their African-Americanization via the same processes as when in their home countries. The same processes hold true outside of America in places like the United Kingdom (UK) where we find a high concentration of Caribbean and Africans who immigrate there looking for better economic opportunities. Their racial-class segregation in the UK leads to similar structural processes and outcomes which impact black America, and the subsequent influence via the global media under American hegemony of black American preachers among adults and hip-hop, athletic, entertainment, hustling culture among the youth leads to the ever-increasing African-Americanization of black British life within the class dynamics of black America.

BLACKS IN THE UNITED KINGDOM (UK)

British blacks come in the main from two racial classes or social class language games, black underclass and bourgeoisie, of the Caribbean and Africa, which discriminated against other practical consciousnesses, transgendered, homosexuality, feminism, etc., arrived-at through the deferment of meaning in ego-centered communicative discourse; the drives of the body; and or impulses of subatomic particles. In Britain, however, these two social class language games, black bourgeoisie and underclass, would come to form one mutually inclusive small (2.5 percent of the total population) but significant black minority community, which is more reminiscent of America than the Caribbean or Africa, constituted as a racial-caste-in-class. Historically, small numbers of Africans have been in Britain since Elizabethan times but it was the development of maritime links with West Africa which led to the growth of a sizeable black population. By the time the early British colonies had gained a foothold in the Caribbean and North America, economic ties had been created via the 'triangular trade.' As the slave industry developed more blacks came to England, some directly from Africa and others via the Americas. Many were resold or bartered in England through advertisements in London (Walvin 1992).

According to the Gentleman's Magazine, there were 20,000 Black people in London in 1764 (Walvin 1984: 33-34). Most of them were poor. Some such as Francis Barber and Olaudah Equiano, rose to fame, whilst others like Billy Water, the one legged fiddler dubbed the King of Beggars, gained notoriety. The treatment of blacks in the late eighteenth and early nineteenth century ranged from brutality to friendship and intimacy. Blacks in London formed their own social and political groups to campaign for the liberation of black slaves and to offer assistance and security. Early contact with Africans set the stage for the racial attitudes which have permeated society in Britain to the present day. As Walvin (1984, pg., 32) explains:

> Europeans had long known of the more exotic people from distant parts of the world ... of the bizarre and strange sights of human nature to be found lurking beyond the pale of European society ... Few offered a more startling contrast to contemporary values of beauty, social virtue and godliness than the Black Africans.

The racism clearly evidenced throughout the Eighteenth Century was oppressive in nature. Britain's economic power, for instance, was dependent on slavery and the attitudes which prevailed sustained the oppression of Black people (Fryer, 1984).

By the Nineteenth Century, the black population had declined. A few slaves returned to Sierra Leone in 1787. They were also shipped to the Caribbean because of the successful campaign against the slave trade in 1807 (mainly brought by Black slaves) and the decline in Britain's interest in the Caribbean, which coincided with expansion to other parts of the globe and the advent of the Industrial Revolution.

Even though the black population decreased, they continued to make a mark on British society. Notable black people included William Curray, the radical Chartist, Ira Aldridge, the famous actor and Mary Seacole, the nurse who tended to the wounds of British soldiers during the Crimean War. Africans also arrived throughout the nineteenth century as students, runaway slaves, or sailors. Black sailors, however, were by far the largest group. They established their roots in British maritime communities such as Cardiff and Liverpool. Blacks also served in the British army during the First World War (cf Fryer, 1984). These blacks were exposed to open discrimination in all aspects of life including the Trade Union Movement. Blacks were criticized for taking work from local whites and also for having sexual relationships with White women – a theme which preoccupies contemporary society (Walvin 1984). By 1921, the repatriation of black people was being widely advocated and within a short period of time, racial hatred was spilling over into riots in Cardiff, Liverpool, and London. Continuing discrimination led ultimately to the foundation of the League of Colored People by the Jamaican Harold Moody in 1931. The anti-imperialistic Pan-African movement emerged in the inter-war period. Black publications, for example, *West Africa and The Keys,* grew in popularity. Other organizations and journals concerned with black issues and freedom in Africa and the Caribbean were also established (Walvin 1984). Black nationalists found political allies in many

British left-wing groups. The Italian invasion of Ethiopia also had an impact on black Nationalism in Britain.

During the early years of the Second World War, black workers were incorporated into the workforce. Britain also opened its doors to a number of different nationalities, including their European neighbors and American soldiers, many of whom were black. There is evidence that Caribbean troops who fought during the war were subjected to similar forms of racial discrimination as those experienced by African-American soldiers in the American army (James, 1980).

POST-WAR MIGRATION

Immediately after World War II, many black soldiers were shipped back to their respective islands; however, some remained and were joined by the first arrival of migrant workers from Jamaica to Britain in June 1948 on the ship *Empire Windrush*, and increasing numbers of Caribbean people subsequently came to Britain to fill the labor gap in the post-war period. In 1951 there were some 15,000 Caribbean newcomers. It is important to mention that America had been the traditional destination for Caribbean people but their entry was restricted because of new legislation, most notably the 1952 McCarren-Warren Act. As a result of the Act, Britain became the natural focus for migration. The early migrants came from islands that had historic links with Britain such as Jamaica, St Kitts, Barbados, and Montserrat. In some cases British organizations such as the London Transport and regional hospital boards launched recruiting drives in the Caribbean (Walvin, 1984). Many Jamaicans, in particular, were recruited through a network of travel agents. In Barbados, the authorities provided loans and assistance for local migrants.

The extent of population movement varied enormously from island to island. In 1960, for example, 9.2 per cent of Jamaican population and 31.5 per cent of Montserratians emigrated to the United Kingdom, but less than 2 per cent of Trinidadians and Tobagans. It is estimated by the Migrant Services Division of the West Indian Federation Office that the total number of Caribbean immigrants entering the United Kingdom in 1961 was 238,000 (Peach 1968, p. 15). Most early immigrants were young men without dependents (Foner, 1979). Later migrants were mainly women and children. Elyse Dodgson (1985 pg., 64) captures some of the experiences of Caribbean women who migrated to Britain during this time:

> Life was much harder for women than it was for men . . . I used to have to take the two children to the child-minder and go to work in the factory – I had to catch the bus at half-past five . . . I come back and use the coal fire. They rent

you a room but you can't do anything . . . sometimes you had to hide the iron . . . You think it is little hardness we suffer in this country.

The 1960s saw the enactment of progressively more stringent legislation on immigration. By the 1970s, mass immigration had virtually come to a halt, following the 1971 Immigration Act which put severe restriction on family reunification and chain migration. The total Caribbean population in Britain was estimated at 1.5 percent of the population by 1971. Contemporarily, well over a third of the current Black population is British born and over half of those who are immigrants have been in Britain for more than 30 years. The overall numbers of new immigrants now arriving in Britain is smaller than the numbers returning to the Caribbean. Recent estimates of the Caribbean population provided by the Statistical bulletin (2011) suggests that there are over 600,000 Black Caribbean people (approximately 1.3 per cent) in Britain, of the total population of 55 million. The African population is estimated to be 0.9 percent of the total population. This translates into around 476,000 people from over 40 different sub-Saharan countries of origin. Hence in the aggregate some 1.5 million blacks, 2.5 percent, constitute the population of the total population of the UK. For the most part, they constitute British society as a racial-caste-in-class dominated by the practical consciousnesses of two social class language games, a black bourgeoisie and working class, which is defined by their Standard British English, church attendance, education, economic status, and upward social mobility in the society, and a black underclass defined by their Black British Talk, single female-headed household, underemployment, poverty, etc. Both groups, for the most part, immigrated to the UK from agricultural and emerging industrial societies under the social class language game of a black bourgeoisie whose language and ideals, as previously mentioned, are those of their former colonial masters as it stands against the language and material conditions of the black poor underclass residing either in rural, agricultural areas or the urban slums of their overcrowded capital cities. Moreover, both groups share the same ideals of economic gain, status, upward mobility, and prestige offered by the global capitalist world-system, and discriminate against practical consciousnesses arrived at through the deferment of meaning in ego-centered communicative discourse, the drives of the body, and impulses of subatomic particles.

IDEOLOGIES, POLICIES AND PRACTICES

Ever since the significant number of black Caribbeans and Africans arrived to Britain they have faced racism at every level of society. This is a direct parallel to the processes that impacted black America. Like their African American counterparts, disproportionate numbers of black people in the UK were categorized as black, Afro-Caribbeans, and faced with the worst features of urban deprivation and indeed suffered from multiple deprivation, primarily in the form of low unemployment, given the relocation of British industrial work to developing countries, bad housing, and of course poor education. Several steps were undertaken since the 1950s, when blacks from the Caribbean began arriving in great numbers, to establish equal treatment of all ethnic groups in Britain. First, the 1965 Race Relations Act banned ethnic discrimination at public places and was followed by the 1968 Race Relations Act which ensured that it was unlawful to discriminate on grounds of color, race, ethnic or national origins in recruitment and terms and conditions of employment (Layton-Henry, 1984). This definition of discrimination was extended in the 1976 Race Relations Act which covered race discrimination in employment and training, housing and education, the provision of goods, facilities and services and advertising and to forms of implicit discrimination in which there is absence of deliberate intention to discriminate. In 2001, the Race Relations Act 2000 (Amendment) was instituted to maintain the provisions of the previous acts and to encourage public authorities to fight discrimination.

THE LABOR MARKET

The labor market was a major area of concern for black Caribbean and African people, and research shows widespread discrimination in this domain. For example, early studies such as the 1974 PEP (Political and Economic Planning) survey described in some detail the position that black workers occupied and the unemployment rates among black people were estimated to be twice as high as those reported for whites. In the 1980s the average length of unemployment for black men, especially those living outside London was considerably higher, and it has been calculated that over half of black unemployed men had registered for over a year, compared with a third of white unemployed men. Similarly, twice as many black women as whites were unemployed over a long period of time (Brown 1985). A study by Troyna & Smith (1983), suggested that high academic qualifications did not guarantee success among black people in the labor market. Neli (2006) argues some studies, particularly those conducted in the 1960s and 1970s, do not clearly categorize between the main different minority groups including Asians (in the UK context Indians, Pakistanis, Bangladeshis) and black (Caribbean and African) although she cites an early study by Neil McIntosh and David Smith (1974) who report that black Caribbean people experienced slightly higher levels of prejudice compared to other ethnic groups. Blacks in the UK are seen homogenously and a distinction is not made sometimes between black Caribbean and black African or indeed between black

Africans who are marked in religion, culture and customs as previously mentioned. Black Caribbean people are from pre-slavery and post-colonial backgrounds whereas many black Africans though coming from colonial countries were not enslaved and their responses to racism tends to be rather different than that of black Caribbeans. In spite of being more educated than their black Caribbean counterparts, which should increase employment possibilities and opportunities, research suggests they often have similar employment prospects to their Caribbean counterparts, however (Berthoud, 2000).

The 1980s and 90s signaled a turning point in the labor market for black people, especially in local councils where there was a visible increase in black employment. This could partly be attributed to the paradigm shift in thinking about race and equality particularly in the 1980s. Notions of multiculturalism and anti-racism and the rise politically of the so-called 'looney-leftist' particularly in certain London boroughs and evidenced in education saw an increase of jobs in the race industry, although both white and blacks benefited from these positions. However, the 1990s presented a similar picture of the previous decade which is confirmed by the Fourth National Survey of Ethnic Minorities in 1994 showing that black Caribbeans experienced high unemployment rates with almost two-thirds of male respondents concentrated in manual labor; further they expressed higher levels of self-reported discrimination than any other minority ethnic group. Over a quarter believed that they had been refused a job on the grounds of their color (Modood et al, 1997).

The labor market throws light on the practices of the ideological notions of integration, and it is assumed that the degree of integration depends on the participatory economic performance of the second generation of the respective minority group. The offspring raised in the host community are often assumed to be more advantageous than their parents and to have reach equity with whites (Chiswick, 1978). Some studies which differentiate between the two generations refute this assumption. Researchers such as Blackaby et al (2005), for example, found that employment rates among second generation black Caribbean men along with Pakistani men were high. Utilizing British survey data Ludi Simpson (2006) compares the 1991 and 2001 Censuses and found the net disadvantage of minority ethnic groups in the labor market has become greater for men born in the UK. Heath and Cheung (2006) report that Caribbean men together with their Pakistani counterparts suffered more disadvantages than other groups in unskilled labor. A recent study by Berthoud (2009) reveals that since the start of the recession, black British people aged 16 to 24 years old have the highest rates of unemployment than any other group at over 48 percent, compared to 20 percent for white young people. Whether these figures can be attributed to the practices of employers is unclear but what is not in doubt is that despite extensive anti-discrimination laws, black Caribbean and African immigrants together with other minority ethnic groups have experienced a negative impact in the labor market profile and they have not achieved parity with native whites. As Neli (2006) argues employers' practices still put certain ethnic groups at a disadvantage (Heath and Yu, 2005). Occupational status and social class background does not render the latter invalid.

As previously mentioned, most Caribbean and African people in Britain historically came from either the upper classes of colored people seeking an education, or working class rural and urban backgrounds and were employed in jobs traditionally assigned to white working class people. Migrants who came from middle class backgrounds in their homelands were also absorbed into white working class occupations. The process of migration often disrupts traditional views of class positions and identities. Migrants in general often experience decreased mobility when they arrive to Britain and often have to work their way up to middle class occupational status (Archer, 2009). Employment opportunities for Blacks during the previous decades had been rather limited, especially for the middle classes, and it is pertinent to ascertain their position in the labor market during the 21st Century. Contemporarily, there are indications that there exists a growing population of African and Caribbean middle classes (Clark & Drinkwater, 2007) reflecting the higher levels of education among this group, often attained after compulsory schooling. Whilst there has been a growing interest in middle class families and their engagement with education (Ball 2003; Power et al 2003; Reay et al 2007), as education is the precursor to high status employment and thereby leading to status attainment, it is largely framed within the context of the white middle classes. Archer (2009) focuses on the tensions in the conception of black Caribbean middle classness in the UK highlighting the 'struggle between dominant discourses that conflate authentic (and 'cool'/popular) blackness with working classness (as both imposed by dominant white society and as articulated from within minority ethnic collectivities) and participants' resistance to 'pretentious' versions of ME [minority ethnic] middle class identity (p. 16). The authentic 'black' middle class in Archer's (2009) study were often constructed as 'out there' – but 'not for me' and there was ambivalence about joining a group which mainly 'functioned as a sort of pariah identity (pg. 17).' This rejection was used to distance the self from the negative aspects of middle classness such as pretense, snobbery including the markers evidenced in the historical elites as opposed to the socially mobile, and as a strategy for managing the challenging identity conflicts experienced by respondents. Archer's findings corroborate Nicola Rollock's (2010) study of black Caribbean heritage middle class families. In exploring the self-identity of class, some participants unequivocally identified themselves as working or middle class but the majority was hesitant and ambivalent about occupying a dual identity that is both black and middle class. We argue that constructs of identities within racialized industrialized European societies such as Britain presents challenges for black individuals born and socialized in Britain where the idea of middle classness and professionalism is synonymous with being white, while poverty, the street life, and black British Talk is seen as the identity marker of so-called "blackness." There is the perception as described by one of the present author's mother, that the professional landscape of Britain is 'bare white' (only white). Working class black individuals in particular do not always distinguish between white working and middle class individuals, particularly if they are in a professional environment; yet there is a perception of white 'chavs' (underclass) who are seen as the equivalent to 'ghetto' that is the black underclass, who are associated with certain behaviors such as black British talk, hustling, (selling cannabis/weed, driving fast cars etc.), and playing sports. Compared to the US there appears to be a dearth of black Caribbean and African professionals in the UK (Johns, 2011). Middle classness or professionalism however, the term is defined, for blacks who have spent most of their teenage or adult life in the Caribbean or Africa represents a norm and aspiration, which contemporarily is being juxtaposed against an emerging black British underclass culture, influenced by the black American underclass hip-hip culture of the US, as a viable means for both status and economic mobility (Mocombe and Tomlin, 2013).

Notwithstanding issues around identity and social class linked to high/low status professions, most African and Caribbean young people as we have seen occupy a lower position in the labor market compared to their white counterparts. Statistical analysis also points to black African and Caribbean people in 'middle-class' occupations facing inequities, reporting lower average earnings and accessing higher positions than their white peers. The gap in the earning potential between white and black and other ethnic groups is even greater in professional and managerial occupations (Clark & Drinkwater 2007).

HOUSING

Coupled with the labor market, the discriminatory housing policies of the 1960s helped create 'immigrant communities' and schools, which has had far-reaching effects on black people in Britain in the twenty-first Century. Then and now, the housing circumstances of black people in Britain are in many ways inferior to those of whites. Blacks tend to occupy less desirable property, whether it is private or council, than whites. Black people tend to be housed because they are homeless whereas whites are more often allocated property for other reasons. The property occupied by black tenants is inferior to that occupied by whites and blacks tend to wait longer for house transfer than whites. Black people tend to have lower earnings and therefore less capital invested in property. The areas they live are perceived as posing problems (Brown 1985 pgs., 78-94). While there is evidence that the housing conditions of black people have improved significantly since their initial settlement in Britain, substantial inequalities between whites and blacks remain (HMSO, 1991).

EDUCATION

The concentration of blacks and other minorities in deprived white inner-city areas where work has disappeared beginning in the 1960s have created huge social and educational challenges which have greatly impacted on the quality of education of future generations of black children. A major concern in the 1960s was the increase in 'colored' settlement at the time as whites moved out (Rex & Moore, 1967) which inevitably saw increases in the number of immigrant children in certain schools and the fear of racial enclaves in those schools. The decentralized educational system at the time responded to the overflow of immigrant children with the Commonwealth Immigrant Advisory Council (CIAC 1964) advising the dispersal of the children on the grounds that the rates at which other children could progress academically and their assimilation into the British way of life. The 1965 DES7/65 Circular that followed on the Education of Immigrants recommended that a class or school should limit their intake of immigrant children to one-third and that local authorities responsible for the provision of education should adopt dispersal between schools. Although only a few local authorities bussed children, the policy was criticized and ruled illegal in 1975 after a court case involving the Race Relations Board and the Ealing Local Education Authority (LEA) (Kogan 1975). In England bussing only involved children from minority ethnic backgrounds and not White children.

The Home Office's grants to local authorities through Section 11 of a 1966 Local Government Act to provide funding for substantial numbers for 'immigrants from the Commonwealth whose language and customs differ from those of the community' (Local Government Act 1966: Section 11) impacted on educational institutions as grant maintained schools and colleges were eligible for such grants. The Local Government Act of 1993 extended the scope of the grant to all minority ethnic people, to address disadvantage brought about by differences of language or culture experienced by members of any ethnic minorities in accessing education, training, employment and a wide range of other opportunities, services and facilities that are available to other people. It has been argued, however, that black African and Caribbean pupils have not greatly benefitted from Section 11 funding (Tomlinson, 2008).

The shift by the state, with the rise of the UK's postindustrial economy, from the language of assimilation to inculcate notions of integration and equal opportunities were to some extent reflected in educational policies such as the Plowden Report (1967) which acknowledged the value of a more child-centred approach to education and the establishment of Educational Priority Areas giving extra funding to education in disadvantaged cities. The demonization of perceived liberality in education during this time coincided with Black Paper publications by right-wing authors such as Cox & Boyson (1997) who subscribed to the deterministic theories of intelligence, popularized by Hans Eysenck & Arthur Jensen (1978). On the one hand, Black Paper authors pathologized the poor, and the majority of blacks who by their economic position were in the poverty category. On the other hand, more liberal policies advocated compensatory education and remedial education to circumvent the cycle and curtail the culture of poverty. Unfortunately, educationalists failed, then and to some extent even now, to draw attention to the macroeconomic conditions that create failure and inequities particularly for many young black people who are positioned by society for exclusion due to race and class. According to Tomlinson (2008, pg., 28),

> in Britain, a first generation of settlers had strong incentives to move towards absorption into a society that appeared to offer social and economic mobility for their children, but soon realized that physical and cultural difference meant a denial of equal educational opportunities, at best through ignorance and naivety on the part of educationalists and at worst through overt and covert discrimination.

The situation of the education of black Caribbean and African pupils in the UK remains a cause for concern. The inability or unwillingness of the British school system to help young black people fulfill their academic potential has been extensively discussed for the past 40 years (REF). This depressing picture, however, is tied to the intersection between the economic structure of British society as prescribed by the American global capitalist social structure of class inequality, and the initiative of black youth, which became constituted as a permanent underclass given the experience of racism and classism in the labor, housing, and education sphere of the society. Hence, contemporarily, just as in the case of US blacks, British blacks are perpetually underachieving vis-à-vis their white counterparts in education as an ideological apparatus for the UK's postindustrial economy. As a result, the majority remain in the social class language game of the black underclass of British inner-cities geographically and socially separated from the social class language game of their more educated professional classes.

In sum, like the black Americans in the US, black African and Caribbean British life was constituted as a racial-caste-in-class, which is an epiphenomenon of their historical experiences within the world and Britain's capitalist social structure of class inequality, differentiated as two social class language games, a black bourgeoisie and underclass. Upon arrival to the UK, from places like Ghana, Nigeria, Democratic Republic of the Congo, Somali, etc., many black Africans became grouped with the blacks from the Caribbean as blacks (Afro-Caribbean) differentiated by their class positions, a more educated middle class of blacks juxtaposed against an underclass of unemployed/uneducated or poorly educated poor blacks searching for an identity in a postindustrial social landscape within the UK in which identity politics has been commodified for capital accumulation. Their achievement or underachievement within education as an ideological apparatus for the British postindustrial economy continues their class differentiation.

Contemporarily, given their similar experiences within the class division of the global capitalist social relations of production, and the process of globalization under American capital hegemony, the identity of British blacks in the UK, as in the case of all blacks around the world, are ever-so slowly being influenced and determined by the racial-class processes of US blacks as divided between the social class language games of a black bourgeoisie under the leadership of black preachers and educated professionals and a poorly educated/uneducated black underclass under the leadership of criminals, rappers, athletes, and entertainers. The racial-class segregation of Caribbean and African blacks in the UK coupled with the influence of black American preachers through their evangelism and televangelism, and urban black American youth criminal, hip-hop, athletic, and entertainment culture, is leading to their African-Americanization just like their counterparts who immigrate to the United States.

THE AFRICAN-AMERICANIZATION OF AFRICA, THE CARIBBEAN, AND THE OVERALL BLACK DIASPORA

The black underclass urban youth criminal, hip-hop, and athletic practical consciousness, in America's ghettoes, an amalgamation of black American and diasporic practical consciousness, has slowly become, since the 1980s, with the financialization of hip-hop culture by record labels such as Sony and others, athletics, and the entertainment industry, the bearers of ideological and linguistic domination for black youth in the black community in America and throughout the globe. Their language and worldview as constituted through the streets, criminals, hip-hop practical consciousness, athletics and the entertainment industry financed by finance capital, has decentered black bourgeois practical consciousness, and become the means by which black American youth (and youth throughout the world) attempt to recursively reorganize and reproduce their material resource framework against the purposive-rationality of black bourgeois or middle class America led by preachers and educated professionals. The upper-class of owners and high-level executives of the American dominated capitalist world-system have capitalized on this through the commodification of black underclass urban culture for postindustrial entertainment industry. This is further supported by an American media and popular culture that glorifies athletes, entertainers, and the "Bling bling," wealth, diamonds, cars, jewelry, and money. Hence the aim of many young blacks in American society is no longer to seek status, economic gain, and upward mobility through a Protestant Ethic that stresses hard work, diligence, differed gratification, and education; on the contrary, sports, music, instant gratification, illegal activities (drug dealing), and skimming are the dominant means portrayed for their efforts through the entertainment industry financed by post-industrial capital. Schools throughout urban American inner cities are no longer seen as means to a professional end in order to obtain economic gain, status, and upward mobility, but obstacles to that end because it delays gratification and is not correlative with the means associated with economic success and upward mobility in black urban America. More black American youth (especially the black male) want to become, football and basketball players, rappers and entertainers, like many of their role models who were raised in their underclass environments and obtained economic gain and upward mobility that way, over doctors, lawyers, engineers, etc., the social functions associated with the status symbol of the black and white middle professional (educated) class of the civil rights generation. Hence the end and social action remains the same, economic success, status, and upward economic mobility, only the means to that end have shifted with the rise, financed by finance capital, of the black underclass as the bearers of ideological and linguistic domination in black America given the commodification of hip-hop culture and their high visibility in the media and charitable works through basketball and football camps and rap concerts, which reinforce the aforementioned activities as viable means to wealth and status in the society's postindustrial economy, which focuses on services and entertainment for the world's transnational bourgeois class as the mode of producing surplus-value.

This linguistic and ideological domination and the ends of the power elites (rappers, athletes, gangsters) of the black underclass, "mismatch of linguistic structure and social function," which brings about the role conflict Ogbu interprets as the burden of acting white, are juxtaposed against the Protestant Ethic and spirit of capitalism of the black middle and upper middle educated professional classes represented in the prosperity discourse and discursive practices of black American preachers in the likes of TD Jakes, Creflo Dollar, Eddie Long, Juanita Bynum, etc. who, through their televangelism, push forth, via the black American church, education and professional jobs as viable means to prosperity, status, and upward economic gain. Hence, whereas, for agents of the Protestant Ethic and the spirit of capitalism in the likes of Jakes, Dollar, Bynum, Eddie Long, and other educated professionals the means to "Bling bling," or the American Dream, is through education and obtaining a professional job as a sign of God's grace, salvation, and blessings; speaking black English, Rapping, hustling, sports, etc., for younger black Americans, Wyclef Jean, Rihanna, Biggie Smalls, etc., growing up in gentrified inner-cities throughout the US, where industrial work has disappeared, represent the means (not education) to the status position of "Bling bling."

So what we are suggesting here is that contemporarily black American youth are not "acting white" when education no longer becomes a priority or the means to economic gain, status, and upward mobility, as they get older and consistently underachieve vis-à-vis whites; they are attempting to be white and achieve bourgeois economic status (the "Bling bling" of cars, diamonds, gold, helicopters, money, etc.) in the society by being "black," speaking Ebonics, rapping, playing sports, hustling, etc., in a racialized post-industrial capitalist social structure wherein the economic status of "blackness" is (over) determined by the white capitalists class of owners and high-level executives and the black proletariats of the West, the black underclass, whose way of life and image ("athletes, hustlers, hip-hopsters") has been commodified (by white and black capitalists) and distributed throughout the world for entertainment, (black) status, and economic purposes in post-industrial capitalist America. This underclass culture as globally promulgated throughout the black diaspora by finance capital via the commodification of black urban youth images (black athletes and entertainers in commercials), Black Entertainment Television (BET), and other media outlets is counterbalanced or opposed by black preachers, gospel artists, and educated professionals promoting the same ethos, The Protestant Ethic and the spirit of capitalism, via the prosperity gospel of the black American churches, to working and middle class blacks around the world via biblical conversion or salvation, over the pathologies of the black American underclass, as the medium to and for success in the capitalist world-system. Hence, the social structure of class (not racial or cultural worldview) inequality that characterizes the black American social environment is subsequently the relational framework, which black youth and the black middle class in the diaspora are exposed to and socialized in when they encounter globalizing processes through immigration, the outsourcing of work from America, and the black American images of the entertainment industry/media industrial complex.

CONCLUSIONS

Throughout the continent of Africa, the Caribbean, and black Europe black American charismatic preachers like TD Jakes, Creflo Dollar, Juanita Bynum, Eddie Long, etc., are promoting a prosperity gospel among the black adult poor and middle class administrators, which is usually juxtaposed against the emergence of an underclass youth culture in these areas influenced by the criminality, hip-hop, and athletic language and culture of the black American underclass (Ntarangwi, 2009). Nigerian, South African, East African, St. Lucian, Jamaican, Haitian, and black British Caribbean Hip-Hop, gangsta rap music, Bling bling, dress code, etc., influenced by the black American underclass are juxtaposed against the Protestant evangelism of Nigerian, South African, East African, St. Lucian, Jamaican, Haitian, and black British Caribbean preachers influenced by the prosperity gospel of TD Jakes, Creflo Dollar, Juanita Bynum, and other black charismatic preachers whose global outreach via TBN, speaking engagements, goodwill ambassadorships, movies, etc., throughout the diaspora are converting other blacks to agents of the Protestant Ethic and the spirit of capitalism via their ministries, which emphasizes Protestant Christian tenets of faith, health, wealth, and prosperity. These two class identities, which emerge out of slavery, colonialism, decolonization, and postindustrial America, the hegemon of globalization, represent the racial-class dynamics within which black others throughout the world are dialectically integrated into the capitalist world-system. In the diaspora, the black underclasses, emulating the black American underclass, seek to commodify their underclass linguistic patois, criminality, musical genres, athletic cultures, and culinary tastes for the tourist markets at home and abroad for status, economic gain, and upward mobility over education. The bourgeoisies of the diaspora, building on the practical consciousness of the black American bourgeoisie, conversely, continue to promote education and entrepreneurships as means to economic gain, status, and upward mobility. Future research in the likes of Mwenda Ntarangwi (2009), who looks at the emergence of East African Hip Hop (Kenya, Uganda, and Tanzania) in his work *East African Hip Hop*, must continue to explore the aforementioned African American class dynamics, led by black American hip hopsters and preachers as the bearers of ideological and linguistic domination, by which other blacks throughout the world are integrated into the capitalist world-system under American hegemony.

References Cited

Adorno, Theodor W. (2000). *Negative Dialectics*. New York: Continuum.
Allen, Ernest Jr. (2002). "Du Boisian Double Consciousness: The Unsustainable Argument." *The Massachusetts Review*, 43 (2): 21 7–253.
Allen, Ernest Jr. (1992). "Ever Feeling One's Twoness: 'Double Ideals and 'Double Consciousness' in the Souls of Black Folk." *Critique of Anthropology*, 12 (3): 26 1–275.
Allen, Richard L. (2001). *The Concept of Self: A Study of Black Identity and Self Esteem*. Detroit: Wayne State University Press.
Alleyne, M. (1980). *Comparative Afro-American*. Ann Arbor: Karoman Press. (1989) *The Roots of Jamaican Culture*. London: Pluto Press.
Althusser, Louis (2001). *Lenin and Philosophy and Other Essays*. New York: Monthly Review Press.
Althusser, Louis and Étienne Balibar (1970). *Reading Capital* (Ben Brewster, Trans.). London: NLB.
Altschuler, Richard (ed.) (1998). *The living Legacy of Marx, Durkheim, and Weber: Applications and Analyses of Classical Sociological Theory by Modern Social Scientists*. New York: Gordian Knot Books.
Appiah, Anthony (1985). "The Uncompleted Argument: Du Bois and the Illusion of Race." *Critical Inquiry*, 12: 2 1–37.
Aptheker, Herbert (ed.) (1985). *W.E.B. Du Bois Against Racism: Unpublished Essays, Papers, Addresses, 188 7–1961*. Amherst: The University of Massachusetts Press.
Archer, Kevin et al (2007). "Locating Globalizations and Cultures." *Globalizations*, 4, 1: 1–14.
Archer, L. (2009) The 'Black' Middle classes and Education: Parents and Young People's Constructions of Identity, Values and Educational Practices. Paper Presented to British Education Research Association (BERA) September. University of Manchester.
Archer, L. (2011) Constructing Minority Ethnic Middle-class identity: An Exploratory Study with Parents, Pupils and Young Professionals. *Sociology* 45 (1): 13 4–151.
Archer, L. & Francis, B. (2007) *Understanding Minority Ethnic Achievement: Race, Gender, Class and 'Success'*. London: Routledge.
Archer, Margaret S. (1985). "Structuration versus Morphogenesis." In H.J. Helle and S.N. Eisenstadt (Eds.), *Macro-Sociological Theory: Perspectives on Sociological Theory* (Volume 1) (pp. 5 8–88). United Kingdom: J.W. Arrowsmith Ltd.
Asante, Molefi Kete (1988). *Afrocentricity*. New Jersey: Africa World.
Asante, Molefi K. (1990a). *Kemet, Afrocentricity and Knowledge*. New Jersey: Africa World.
Austin, J.L. (1997). *How to do Things With Words* (Second edition, J.O. Urmson and Marina Sbisà, editors). Cambridge, Massachusetts: Harvard University Press.
Bailey, B.L. (1966). *Jamaican Creole Syntax*. Cambridge: Cambridge University Press.

References Cited

Baker, Houston A., Jr. (1985). "The Black Man of Culture: W.E.B. Du Bois and The Souls of Black Folk." In William L. Andrews (Ed.), *Critical Essays on W.E.B. Du Bois* (pp.12 9–139). Boston: G.K. Hall & Co.

Balibar, Etienne & Immanuel Wallerstein (1991 [1988]). *Race, Nation, Class: Ambiguous Identities.* London: Verso.

Ballantine, Jeanne, H. (1993). *The Sociology of Education: A systematic Analysis* (3rd Edition). New Jersey: Prentice Hall.

Barone, C. (2006). Cultural Capital, Ambition and the Explanation of Inequalities in Learning Outcomes: A Comparative Analysis. *Sociology*, 40 (6): 1039–1058.

Barrs, M. and Cork, V. (2001). *The Reader in the Writer: The Links between the Study of Literature and Writing Development at Key Stage 2.* London: Centre for Language in Primary Education.

Barthes, Roland (1972). *Mythologies* (Annette Lavers, Trans.). New York: Hill and Wang.

Bashi, V and Hughes, M. (1997). Globalization and Residential Segregation by 'Race.' *Annuls of the American Academy of Social and Political Science*, 551: 10 5–20.

Beauvoir, Max (2006). "Herbs and Energy: The Holistic Medical System of the Haitian People." In Bellegarde-Smith, Patrick and Claudine Michel (eds.) *Haitian Vodou: Spirit, Myth, & Reality* (pgs. 11 2–133). Bloomington, IN: Indiana University Press.

Bellegarde-Smith, Patrick and Claudine Michel (2006). *Haitian Vodou: Spirit, Myth, & Reality.* Bloomington, IN: Indiana University Press.

Bell, Daniel (1985). *The Social Sciences Since the Second World War.* New Brunswick (USA): Transaction Books.

Bell, Bernard W. et al (editors) (1996). *W. E. B. Du Bois on Race and Culture: Philosophy, Politics, and Poetics.* New York and London: Routledge.

Bell, Bernard W. (1996). "Genealogical Shifts in Du Bois's Discourse on Double Consciousness as the Sign of African American Difference." In Bernard W. Bell et al (Eds.), *W.E.B. Du Bois on Race and Culture: Philosophy, Politics, and Poetics* (pp. 8 7–108). New York and London: Routledge.

Bell, Bernard W. (1985). "W.E.B. Du Bois's Struggle to Reconcile Folk and High Art." In William L. Andrews (Ed.), *Critical Essays on W.E.B. Du Bois* (pp.10 6–122). Andrews. Boston: G.K. Hall & Co.

Bennett, Lerone (1982). *Before the Mayflower.* Chicago: Johnson PublishingCompany.

Bernstein, B. (1971) *Class, Codes and Control.* New York: Schocken Books.

Berthoud, R. (2000) Ethnic Employment Penalties in Britain. *Journal of Ethnic and Migration Studies*. 26 (3): pp. 38 9–416.

Bhabha, Homi (1995a). "Cultural Diversity and Cultural Differences." In Bill Ashcroft et al (Eds.), *The Post-colonial Studies Reader* (pp. 20 6–209). London and New York: Routledge.

Bhabha, Homi (1995b). "Signs Taken for Wonders." In Bill Ashcroft et al (Eds.), *The Post-colonial Studies Reader* (pp. 2 9–35). London and New York: Routledge.

Bhabha, Homi (1994). "Remembering Fanon: Self, Psyche and the Colonial Condition." In Patrick Williams and Laura Chrisman (Eds.), *Colonial Discourse and Post-Colonial Theory A Reader* (pp. 11 2–123). New York: Columbia University Press.

Bickerton, D. (1975). *Dynamics of a Creole System.* Cambridge: Cambridge University Press.

Billingsley, Andrew (1968). *Black Families in White America.* New Jersey: Prentice Hall.

Billingsley, Andrew (1970). "Black Families and White Social Science." *Journal of Social Issues*, 26, 12 7–142.

Billingsley, Andrew (1993). *Climbing Jacob's Ladder: The Enduring Legacy of African American Families.* New York: Simon & Schuster.

Bizzell, Patricia and Bruce Herzberg (2001). *The Rhetorical Tradition: Readings from Classical Times to the Present.* Boston: Bedford/St. Martin's.

Blackaby, D.H, Leslie, D.G.& Murphy, :D. (2005) N. C. O'Leary Born in Britain: How Are Native Ethnic Minorities faring in the British Labor Market? *Economic Letters* 88 (3): 370–375.

Blassingame, John W. (1972). *The Slave Community: Plantation Life in the Antebellum South.* New York: Oxford University Press.

Bleich, E. (2003) *Race and Politics in Britain and France: Ideas and Policy-making since the 1960s*. Cambridge: Cambridge University Press.

Boskin, Joseph (1965). "Race Relations in Seventeenth-Century America: The Problem of the Origins of Negro Slavery." In Donald Noel (Ed.), *The Origins of American Slavery and Racism* (pp. 9 5–105). Ohio: Charles E. Merrill Publishing Co.

Boswell, Terry (1989). "Colonial Empires and the Capitalist World-Economy: A Time Series Analysis of Colonization, 164 0–1960." *American Sociological Review*, 54, 18 0–196.

Bourdieu, Pierre (1984). *Distinction: A Social Critique of the Judgement of Taste* (Richard Nice, Trans.). Cambridge MA: Harvard University Press.

Bourdieu, P. (1986). The Forms of Capital. In J.E. Richardson (Ed.), *Handbook of Theory and Research for the Sociology of Education* (pp. 241–258). Westport: Greenwood Press.

Bourdieu, Pierre (1990). *The Logic of Practice* (Richard Nice, Trans.). Stanford, California: Stanford University Press.

Boxill, Bernard R. (1996). "Du Bois on Cultural Pluralism." In Bell W. Bernard et al (Eds.), *W.E.B. Du Bois on Race and Culture: Philosophy, Politics, and Poetics* (pp. 5 7–86). New York and London: Routledge.

Brathwaite, E. (1984). *History of the Voice*. London: New Beacon Books.

Brecher, Jeremy and Tim Costello (1998). *Global Village or Global Pillage: Economic Reconstruction from the bottom up* (second ed.). Cambridge, Mass.: South End Press.

Brennan, Teresa (1997). "The Two Forms of Consciousness." *Theory Culture & Society*, 14 (4): 8 9–96.

Broderick, Francis L. (1959). *W.E.B. Du Bois, Negro Leader in a Time of Crisis*. Stanford, California: Stanford University Press.

Brown, C. (1985) *Black and White Britain*. London: Policy Studies Institute.

Bruce, Dickinson D., Jr. (1992). "W.E.B. Du Bois and the Idea of Double Consciousness." *American Literature*, 64: 29 9–309.

Bryne, D. (2001) *Understanding the Urban*. London: Palgrave.

Buck-Morss, Susan (2009). *Hegel, Haiti, and Universal History*. Pittsburgh: University of Pittsburgh Press.

Bullock Report (1975). *A Language for Life*. London. HMSO.

Byron, M. (1994) Post-war Caribbean Migration to Britain. The Unfinished Cycle. Aldershot: Avebury.

Carrington, L.D. (2001). The status of Creole in the Caribbean. In P. Christie (Ed.), *Due Respect: Papers on English and English-Related Creoles in the Caribbean in Honor of Professor Robert Le Page* (pp. 2 4–36). Mona, Kingston: University of the West Indies Press.

Caws, Peter (1997). *Structuralism: A Philosophy for the Human Sciences*. New York: Humanity Books.

Chanda-Goo, S. (2006) *South Asian Communities; Catalysts for Educational Change*. Stoke-on-Trent: Trentham.

Chase-Dunn, Christopher and Peter Grimes (1995). "World-Systems Analysis." *Annual Review of Sociology*, 21, 38 7–417.

Chase-Dunn, Christopher and Richard Rubinson (1977). "Toward a Structural Perspective on the World-System." *Politics & Society*, 7: 4, 45 3–476.

Chase-Dunn, Christopher (1975). "The effects of international economic dependence on development and inequality: A cross-national study." *American Sociological Review*, 40, 72 0–738.

Chiswick, B. (1978) The effect of Americanization on the Earnings of Foreign Born Men. *Journal of Political Economy*, 86 (5), pp.89 7–922.

Christie, P. (2003). *Language in Jamaica*. Kingston, Jamaica: Arawak.

Clark, K and Drinkwater, S. (2007) *Ethnic Minorities in the Labor Market: Dynamics and Diversity*. Abingdon: Joseph Rowntree Foundation. Policy Press.

Clark, Robert P. (1997). *The Global Imperative: An Interpretive History of the Spread of Humankind*. Boulder, Colorado: Westview Press.

Clarke, John Henrik, et. al. (eds.) (1970). *Black Titan: W.E.B. Du Bois*. Boston: Beacon Press.

Clark, P. (1988) *Prejudice and Your Child*. Middletown, Connecticut: Wesleyan University Press.
Coard, B. (1971) *How the Education West Indian Child is Made Educationally Subnormal in the British School System: The Scandal of the Black Child in School*. London: New Beacon Books.
Cohen, J. (2002). *Protestantism and Capitalism: The Mechanisms of Influence*. New York: Aldine de Gruyter.
Cole, M. (2011) Racism and Education in the UK and US. Palgrave Macmillan. New York.
Collinson, Diane (1987). *Fifty Major Philosophers: A Reference Guide*. London:Routledge.
Coser, Lewis (1956). *The functions of social conflict*. New York: The Free Press.
Covino, William A. and David A. Jolliffe (1995). *Rhetoric: concepts, definitions, boundaries*. Needham Heights, Massachusetts: Allyn and Bacon.
Cox, C.B. and Boyson, R. (1977) *Black Paper 1977*. London: Temple-Smith.
Craig, D.R. (1976). Bidialectal education: Creole and Standard in the West Indies. *IJSL* 8: 93–134.
Crosley, Reginald O. (2006). "Shadow-Matter Universes in Haitian and Dagara Ontologies: A Comparative Study." In Bellegarde-Smith, Patrick and Claudine Michel (eds.) *Haitian Vodou: Spirit, Myth, & Reality* (pgs. 7–18). Bloomington, IN: Indiana University Press.
Crothers, Charles (2003). "Technical Advances in General Sociological Theory: The Potential Contribution of Post-Structurationist Sociology." *Perspectives*, 26: (3), 3–6. Crouch, Stanley (1993). "Who are We? Where Did We Come From? Where Are We Going?" In Gerald Early (Ed.), *Lure and Loathing: Essays on Race, Identity, and the Ambivalence of Assimilation* (pp. 8 0–94). New York: The Penguin Press.
Culler, Jonathan (1976). *Saussure*. Great Britain: Fontana/Collins.
Curtin, Philip D. (1969). *The Atlantic Slave Trade: A Census*. Madison, Wisconsin: The University of Wisconsin Press.
Dahrendorf, Ralf (1959). *Class and Class Conflict in Industrial Society*. Stanford, California: Stanford University Press.
Dayan, Joan (1998). Haiti, History, and the Gods. Berkeley and Los Angeles: University of California Press.
Degler, Carl N. (1972). "Slavery and the Genesis of American Race Prejudice." In Donald Noel (Ed.), *The Origins of American Slavery and Racism* (pp. 5 9–80). Ohio: Charles E. Merrill Publishing Co.
DeMarco, Joseph P. (1983). *The Social Thought of W.E.B. Du Bois*. Lanham, MD: University Press of America.
Deren, Maya (1972). *The Divine Horsemen: The Voodoo Gods of Haiti*. New York: Delta Publishing Co.
Desmangles, Leslie G. (1992). *The Faces of the Gods: Vodou and Roman Catholicism in Haiti*. Chapel Hill: The University of North Carolina Press.
Devonish, H. (1986). *Language and Liberation: Creole Language Politics in the Caribbean*. London: Karia Press.
Diop, Cheikh A. (1981). *Civilization or Barbarism: An Authentic Anthropology*. New York: Lawrence Hill Books.
Diop, Cheikh A. (1988). *Precolonial Black Africa*. Chicago: Chicago Review Press.
Diop, Cheikh A. (1989). *The African Origin of Civilization: Myth or Reality*. Chicago: Chicago Review Press.
Dogson, E. (1986) *Motherland: West Indian Women to Britain in the 1950s*. London: Heinemann Education Books.
Douglas, M. (1986). *How Institutions Think*. New York: Syracuse University Press.
Drake, St. Claire (1965). "The Social and Economic Status of the Negro in the United States." In Talcott Parsons and Kenneth B. Clark (Eds.), *The Negro American* (pp. 3–46). Boston: Houghton Mifflin Company.
Du Bois, Laurent (2004). *Avengers of the New World: The Story of the Haitian Revolution*. Cambridge, Massachusetts: Harvard University Press.
Du Bois, Laurent (2012). Haiti: The Aftershocks of History. New York: Metropolitan Books.
Du Bois, W.E.B. (1995 [1903]). *The Souls of Black Folk*. New York: Penguin Putnam Inc.

Du Bois, W.E.B. (1984 [1940]). *Dusk of Dawn: An Essay toward an Autobiography of a Race Concept*. New Brunswick and London: Transaction Books.
Du Bois, W.E.B. (1971a [1897]). "The Conservation of Races." In Julius Lester (Ed.), *The Seventh Son: The Thought and Writings of W.E.B. Du Bois* (Volume I) (pp. 17 6–187). New York: Random House.
Du Bois, W.E.B. (1971b [1935]). "A Negro Nation Within The Nation." In Julius Lester (Ed.), *The Seventh Son: The Thought and Writings of W.E.B. Du Bois* (Volume II) (pp. 39 9–407). New York: Random House.
Du Bois, W.E.B. (1970 [1939]). *Black Folk, Then and Now: An Essay in the History and Sociology of the Negro Race*. New York: Octagon Books.
Du Bois, W. E. B. (1968). *The Autobiography of W.E.B. Du Bois: A Soliloquy on Viewing My Life from the Last Decade of its First Century*. US: International Publishers Co., Inc.
Du Bois, W.E.B. (1967 [1899]). *The Philadelphia Negro: A Social Study*. New York: Schocken Books.
Dupuy, Alex (1989). *Haiti in the World Economy: Class, Race, and Underdevelopment Since 1700*. Boulder, CO: Westview Press.
Durkheim, Emile (1984 [1893]). *The Division of Labor in Society* (W.D. Halls, Trans.).New York: The Free Press.
Eagleton, Terry (1999). *Marx*. New York: Routledge.
Eagleton, Terry (1991). *Ideology: An Introduction*. London: Verso.
Early, Gerald (ed.) (1993). *Lure and Loathing: Essays on Race, Identity, and the Ambivalence of Assimilation*. New York: The Penguin Press.
Edgar, Andrew and Peter Sedgwick (Eds.) (1999). *Key Concepts in Cultural Theory*. London: Routledge.
Economic and Social Survey (2001). Jamaica: Planning Institute of Jamaica.
Elkins, Stanley (1959). *Slavery: A Problem in American Institutional and Intellectual Life*. Chicago: University of Chicago Press.
Elkins, Stanley M. (1972). "The Dynamics of Unopposed Capitalism." In Donald Noel (Ed.), *The Origins of American Slavery and Racism* (pp. 4 5–58). Ohio: Charles E. Merrill Publishing Co.
Engels, Frederick (2000 [1884]. *The Origin of the Family, Private Property, and the State*. New York: Pathfinder Press.
Fanon, Frantz (1967). *Black Skin, White Masks* (Charles Lam Markmann, Trans.). New York: Grove Press.
Fanon, Frantz (1963). *The Wretched of the Earth* (Constance Farrington, Trans). New York: Grove Press.
Fick, Carolyn E. (1990). *The Making of Haiti: The Saint Domingue Revolution from Below*. Knoxville, Tennessee: The University of Tennessee Press.
Fleurant, Gerdés (2006). "Vodun, Music, and Society in Haiti: Affirmation and Identity." In Bellegarde-Smith, Patrick and Claudine Michel (eds.) *Haitian Vodou: Spirit, Myth, & Reality* (pgs. 4 5–57). Bloomington, IN: Indiana University Press.
Fogel, Robert W. (2003). *The Slavery Debates, 195 2–1990: A Retrospective*. Baton Rouge: Louisiana State University Press.
Foner, Eric (1988). *Reconstruction: America's Unfinished Revolution 186 3–1877*. New York: Harper&Row Publishers. .
Foner, Eric (1990). *A Short History of Reconstruction 186 3–1877*. New York: Harper & Row Publishers .
Foner, P. (1979) *Jamaica Farewell*. Jamaican Migrants in London: London: Routledge Kegan & Paul.
Foucault, Michel (1977). *Discipline and Punish: The Birth of the Prison* (Alan Sheridan, Trans.). London: Penguin Books.
Franklin, John Hope and Alfred A. Moss Jr. (2000). *From Slavery to Freedom: A History of African Americans* (Eighth Edition). New York: Alfred A. Knopf.
Fraser, Nancy (1997). *Justice Interruptus: Critical Reflections on the "Postsocialist" Condition*. New York & London: Routledge.

Frazier, Franklin E. (1939). *The Negro Family in America*. Chicago: University of Chicago Press.
Frazier, Franklin E. (1957). *Black Bourgeoisie: The Rise of a New Middle Class*. New York: The Free Press.
Frazier, Franklin E. (1968). *The Free Negro Family*. New York: Arno Press and The New York Times.
Freud, Sigmund (1989 [1940]. *An Outline of Psycho-Analysis* (James Strachey, Trans. and Editor). New York: W.W. Norton & Company.
Freud, Sigmund (1989 [1921]. *Group Psychology and the Analysis of the Ego* (James Strachey, Trans. and Editor). New York: W.W. Norton & Company.
Freud, Sigmund (1989 [1917]. *Introductory Lectures on Psycho-Analysis* (James Strachey, Trans. and Editor). New York: W.W. Norton & Company.
Fryer, P. (1984) *Staying Power: The History of Black People in Britain*. London: Pluto Press.
Gadamer, Hans-Georg (2002). *Truth and Method* (Second, Revised Edition, Joel Weinsheimer and Donald G. Marshall, Trans.). New York: Continuum.
Gartman, David (2002). "Bourdieu's Theory of Cultural Change: Explication, Application, Critique." *Sociological Theory* 20 (2): 25 5–277.
Gates, Henry L. et al. (Eds.) (1997). *The Norton Anthology: African AmericanLiterature* . New York: W.W. Norton & Company Inc.
Gates, Henry Louis, Jr. and Cornel West (1996). *The Future of the Race*. New York: Vintage Books.
Gilroy, P. (1990) 'The end of Anti-Racism.' *New Community*. 17 (1): pp. 7 1–83.
Geertz, Clifford (1973). *The Interpretation of Cultures*. New York: Basic Books.
Geertz, Clifford (2000). *Local Knowledge: Further Essays in Interpretive Anthropology*. New York: Basic Books.
Genovese, Eugene (1974). *Roll, Jordan, Roll*. New York: Pantheon Books.
Geronimus, Arline T. and F. Phillip Thompson. "To Denigrate, Ignore, or Disrupt: Racial Inequality in Health and the Impact of a Policy-induced Breakdown of African American Communities." *Du Bois Review* 1; 2: 24 7–279.
Giddens, Anthony (1984). *The Constitution of Society: Outline of the Theory of Structuration*. Cambridge: Polity Press.
Gilroy, Paul (1987) *There Ain't no Blacks in the Union Jack: The Cultural Politics of Race and Nation*. London: Routledge.
Gilroy, Paul (1993). *The Black Atlantic: Modernity and Double Consciousness*. Cambridge, Massachusetts: Harvard.
Glazer, Nathan and Daniel P. Moynihan (1963). *Beyond the Melting Pot*. Cambridge: Harvard University Press.
Gooding-Williams, Robert (1996). "Outlaw, Appiah, and Du Bois's "The Conservation of Races." In Bell W. Bernard et al. (Eds.), *W.E.B. Du Bois on Race and Culture: Philosophy, Politics, and Poetics* (pp. 3 9–56). New York and London: Routledge.
Gramsci, Antonio (1959). *The Modern Prince, and Other Writings*. New York: International Publishers.
Greene, Joshua (2013). *Moral Tribes: Emotion, Reason, and the Gap Between Us and Them*. New York: The Penguin Press.
Greene, M. & Way, N. (2005) Self-Esteem Trajectories among Ethnic Minority Adolescents: A Growth Curve Analysis of the Patterns and Predictors of Change. *Journal of Research on Adolescence*, (15), 151–178.
Grutter v. Bollinger et al, 539 U.S. 0 2–241 (2003); 13 (Slip Opinion).
Gutiérrez, Ramón A. (2004). "Internal Colonialism: An American Theory of Race." *Du Bois Review*, 1; 2: 28 1–295.
Gutman, Herbert (1976). *The Black Family in Slavery and Freedom 175 0–1925*. New York: Pantheon Books.
Habermas, Jürgen (1987). *The Theory of Communicative Action: Lifeworld and System: A Critique of Functionalist Reason* (Volume 2, Thomas McCarthy, Trans.). Boston: Beacon Press.

Habermas, Jürgen (1984). *The Theory of Communicative Action: Reason and the Rationalization of Society* (Volume 1, Thomas McCarthy, Trans.). Boston: Beacon Press.
Handlin, Oscar and Mary F. Handlin (1972). "The Origins of Negro Slavery." In Donald Noel (Ed.), *The Origins of American Slavery and Racism* (pp. 2 1–44). Ohio: Charles E. Merrill Publishing Co.
Harding, Vincent (1981). *There is a River: The Black Struggle for Freedom in America*. New York: Harcourt Brace & Company.
Hare, Nathan (1991). *The Black Anglo-Saxons*. Chicago: Third World Press.
Harris, Marvin. (1999). *Theories of culture in postmodern times.* Walnut Creek, California: AltaMira Press.
Harris, David R. and Jeremiah Joseph Sim (2002). "Who is Multiracial? Assessing the Complexity of Lived Race." *American Sociological Review* 67; 4: 61 4–627.
Heath, A. and Cheung, S. (2006) *Ethnic Penalties in the Labor Market: Employers and Discrimination.* Research report No 341. London: Department of Work and Pensions.
Heath, A. and Yu, S. (2005) *Explaining Ethnic Minority Disadvantage* (pp.18 7–224). In: Heath, A., Ermisch, J. and Gallie, D. *Understanding social change.* Oxford, Oxford University Press.
Hegel, G.W.F. (1977 [1807]). *Phenomenology of Spirit* (A.V. Miller, Trans.). Oxford: Oxford University Press.
Heidegger, Martin (1962 [1927]). *Being and Time.* New York: Harper SanFrancisco.
Helle, H.J. and S.N. Eisenstadt (ed.) (1985). *Macro-Sociological Theory: Perspectives on Sociological Theory* (Volume 1). United Kingdom: J.W. Arrowsmith Ltd.
Helle, H.J. and S.N. Eisenstadt (ed.) (1985). *Micro-Sociological Theory: Perspectives on Sociological Theory* (Volume 2). United Kingdom: J.W. Arrowsmith Ltd.
Herskovits, Melville J. (1958 [1941]). *The Myth of the Negro Past.* Boston: Beacon Press.
Hewitt, R. (1986) *White Talk Black Talk: Inter-Racial Friendship and Communication amongst Adolescents.* Cambridge: Cambridge University Press.
Hiro, D. (1973*)* *Black British, White British*. Harmondsworth: Penguin.
HMSO (1991) *Aspects of Britain's Ethnic Minorities*. London: H.M.S.O.
Hochschild, Jennifer L. (1984). *The New American Dilemma: Liberal Democracy and School Desegregation.* New Haven: Yale University Press.
Hogue, Lawrence W. (1996). *Race, Modernity, Postmodernity: A look at the History and the Literatures of People of Color Since the 1960s.* Albany: State University of New York Press.
Holloway, Joseph E. (ed.) (1990a). *Africanisms in American Culture*. Bloomington and Indianapolis: Indiana University Press.
Holloway, Joseph E. (1990b). "The Origins of African-American Culture." In Joseph Holloway (Ed.), *Africanisms in American Culture* (1 9–33). Bloomington and Indianapolis: Indiana University Press.
Holt, Thomas (1990). "The Political Uses of Alienation: W.E.B. Du Bois on Politics, Race, and Culture, 190 3–1940." *American Quarterly* 42 (2): 30 1–323.
Horkheimer, Max and Theodor W. Adorno (2000 [1944]). *Dialectic of Enlightenment* (John Cumming, Trans.). New York: Continuum.
Horne, Gerald (1986). *Black and Red: W.E.B. Du Bois and the Afro-American Response to the Cold War, 194 4–1963*. New York: State University of New York Press.
House, James S. (1977). "The Three Faces of Social Psychology." *Sociometry* 40: 16 1–177.
House, James S. (1981). "Social Structure and Personality." In Morris Rosenberg and Ralph Turner (Eds.), *Sociological Perspectives on Social Psychology* (pp. 52 5–561). New York: Basic Books.
Hudson, Kenneth and Andrea Coukos (2005). "The Dark Side of the Protestant Ethic: A Comparative Analysis of Welfare Reform." *Sociological Theory* 23 (1): 1–24.
Hunton, Alphaeus w. (1970). "W.E.B. Du Bois: the meaning of his life." In John Henrik Clarke et al (Eds.), *Black Titan: W.E.B. Du Bois* (pp. 13 1–137). Boston: Beacon Press.
Inkeles, Alex (1959). "Personality and Social Structure." In Robert K. Merton, Leonard Broom, and Leonard S. Cottrell, Jr. (eds.), *Sociology Today* (pp. 24 9–276). New York: Basic Books.

Inkeles, Alex (1960). "Industrial man: The Relation of Status, Experience, and Value." *American Journal of Sociology* 66: 1–31.

Inkeles, Alex (1969). "Making Men Modern: On the causes and consequences of individual change in six developing countries." *American Journal of Sociology* 75: 20 8–225.

James, C.L.R., Breitman, G. & Keemer, E. (1980) Fighting Racism in World War 1. New York: Monad Press.

James, CLR (1986). *The Black Jacobins: Toussaint L' Ouverture and the San Domingo Revolution*. Vintage.

Jameson, Fredric and Masao Miyoshi (ed.). (1998). *The Cultures of Globalization*. Durham: Duke University Press.

Jones, G.S. (1971). *Outcast London: A Study in the Relationship Between Classes in Victorian Society*. Oxford: Clarendon Press.

Jordan, Winthrop D. (1972). "Modern Tensions and the Origins of American Slavery." In Donald Noel (Ed.), *The Origins of American Slavery and Racism* (pp. 8 1–94). Ohio: Charles E. Merrill Publishing Co.

Kardiner, Abram and Lionel Ovesey (1962 [1951]. *The Mark of Oppression: Explorations in the Personality of the American Negro*. Meridian Ed.

Karenga, Maulana (1993). *Introduction to Black Studies*. California: The University of Sankore Press.

Kellner, Douglas (2002). "Theorizing Globalization." *Sociological Theory*, 20: (3), 28 5–305.

Klak, Thomas (Ed.) (1998). *Globalization and Neoliberalism: The Caribbean Context*. Lanham: Rowman & Littlefield Publishers, Inc.

Kneller, George F. (1964). *Introduction to the Philosophy of Education*. New York: John Wiley & Sons, Inc.

Kuhn, Thomas S. (1996). *The Structure of Scientific Revolutions* (Third Edition). Chicago: The University of Chicago Press.

Laclau, Ernesto and Chantal Mouffe (1985). *Hegemony & Socialist Strategy: Towards a Radical Democratic Politics*. New York and London: Verso.

Layton-Henry, Z. (1984) *The Politics of Race in Britain*. London: Allen & Unwin.

Lester, Julius (ed.) (1971). *The Seventh Son: The Thought and Writings of W.E.B. Du Bois* (Volume I). New York: Random House.

Lester, Julius (ed.) (1971). *The Seventh Son: The Thought and Writings of W.E.B. Du Bois* (Volume II). New York: Random House.

Lewis, David Levering (1993). *W.E.B. Du Bois: Biography of a Race 186 8–1919*. New York: Henry Holt and Company.

Levine, Lawrence W. (1977). *Black Culture and Black Consciousness: Afro-American Folk Thought from Slavery to Freedom*. New York: Oxford University Press.

Lévi-Strauss, Claude (1963). *Structural Anthropology* (Claire Jacobson and Brooke Schoepf, Trans.). New York: Basic Books.

Lincoln, Eric C. and Lawrence H. Mamiya (1990). *The Black Church in the African American Experience*. Durham and London: Duke University Press.

Lowenthal, D. (1972) *West Indian Societies*. Oxford: Oxford University Press. Luckmann, Thomas (Ed.) (1978). *Phenomenology and Sociology: Selected Readings*. New York: Penguin Books.

Lukács, Georg (1971). *History and Class Consciousness: Studies in Marxist Dialectics* (Rodney Livingstone, Trans.). Cambridge, Massachusetts: The MIT Press.

Lukács, Georg (2000). *A Defence of History and Class Consciousness: Tailism and the Dialectic* (Esther Leslie, Trans.). London and New York: Verso.

Luscombe, David (1997). *A History of Western Philosophy: Medieval Thought*. Oxford: Oxford University Press.

Lyman, Stanford M. (1997). *Postmodernism and a Sociology of the Absurd and OtherEssays on the "Nouvelle Vague" in American Social Science*. Fayetteville: TheUniversity of Arkansas Press.

Lyman, Stanford M. and Arthur J. Vidich (1985). *American Sociology: Worldly Rejections of Religion and Their Directions*. New Haven and London: Yale University Press.

Lyman, Stanford M. (1972). *The Black American in Sociological Thought*. New York.

Mageo, Jeannette Marie (1998). *Theorizing Self in Samoa: Emotions, Genders, andSexualities*. Ann Arbor: The University of Michigan Press.
Massey, D.S., and Denton, N.A. (1993). *American Apartheid: Segregation and the Making of the Underclass*. Cambridge, MA: Harvard University Press.
Marable, Manning (1986). *W.E.B. Du Bois: Black Radical Democrat*. Boston: Twayne Publishers.
Marcuse, Herbert (1964). *One-Dimensional Man*. Boston: Beacon Press.
Marcuse, Herbert (1974). *Eros and Civilization: A Philosophical Inquiry into Freud*. Boston: Beacon Press.
Marshall, Gordon (Ed.) (1998). *A Dictionary of Sociology* (Second edition). Oxford: Oxford University Press.
Martin, R. and Rowthorn, R, (Eds.) (1986) The Geography of Deindustrialization, London: Macmillan.
Marx, Karl and Friedrich Engels (1964). *The Communist Manifesto*. London, England: Penguin Books.
Marx, Karl (1992 [1867]). *Capital: A Critique of Political Economy* (Volume 1, Samuel Moore and Edward Aveling, Trans.). New York: International Publishers.
Marx, Karl (1998 [1845]). *The German Ideology*. New York: Prometheus Books.
Mason, Patrick L. (1996). "Race, Culture, and the Market." *Journal of Black Studies*, 26: 6, 78 2–808.
Mead, George Herbert (1978 [1910]). "What Social Objects Must Psychology Presuppose." In Thomas Luckmann (Ed.), *Phenomenology and Sociology: Selected Readings* (1 7–24). New York: Penguin Books.
Meier, August (1963). *Negro Thought in America, 188 0–1915: Racial Ideologies in the Age of Booker T. Washington*. Ann Arbor: The University of Michigan Press.
Meier, August and Elliott M. Rudwick (1976 [1966]). *From Plantation to Ghetto; an Interpretive History of American Negroes*. New York: Hill and Wang.
Métraux, Alfred (1958 [1989]). *Voodoo in Haiti*. New York: Pantheon Books.
Michel, Claudine (2006). Of Worlds Seen and Unseen: The Educational Character of Haitian Vodou." In Bellegarde-Smith, Patrick and Claudine Michel (eds.) *Haitian Vodou: Spirit, Myth, & Reality* (pgs. 3 2–44). Bloomington, IN: Indiana University Press.
McMichael, Philip (2008). Development and Social Change: A Global Perspective. Los Angeles, California: Sage Publications.
Milner, D. (1975) *Children and Race*. Harmondsworth: Penguin.
Mirza, H. (2005) The more things change, the more they stay the same: Assessing Black Underachievement 35 years on. In B Richardson. (Ed.) *Tell it like it is. How our School fail Black Children* (pp.11 1–119). Stoke-on-Trent: Trentham Books.
Mocombe, Paul C., Carol Tomlin, Cecile Wright (2014). *Race and Class Distinctions Within Black Communities: A Racial Caste in Class*. Routledge Research in Race and Ethnicity (Vol. 9). New York and London: Routledge.
Mocombe, Paul C., Carol Tomlin, and Cecile Wright (2014). "A Racial Caste in Class: Race and Class Distinctions within Black Communities in the United States and United Kingdom." *Race, Gender, & Class*, 21, 3–4: 10 1–121.
Mocombe, Paul C., Carol Tomlin, and Cecile Wright (2014). "Race and Class Distinctions within Black Communities in the United States and United Kingdom: A Reading in Phenomenological Structuralism." *African and Black Diaspora: An International Journal*.
Mocombe, Paul C., Carol Tomlin, and Victoria Showunmi (2014). "Jesus and the Streets: A Hermeneutical Framework for Understanding the Intraracial Gender Academic Achievement Gap in Black Urban America and the United Kingdom." *Language and Sociocultural Theory*, 1, 2: 12 5–152.
Mocombe, Paul C., Carol Tomlin, and Cecile Wright (2014). "A Structural Approach to Understanding Black British Caribbean Academic Underachievement in the United Kingdom." *Journal of Social Science for Policy Implications*, 2, 2: 3 7–58.
Mocombe, Paul C., Carol Tomlin, and Cecile Wright (2013). "Karl Marx, Ludwig Wittgenstein, and Black Underachievement in the United States and United Kingdom." *Diaspora, Indigenous, and Minority Education*, 7, 4: 21 4–228.

Mocombe, Paul C., Carol Tomlin, and Cecile Wright (2013). "Postindustrial Capitalism, Social Class Language Games, and Black Underachievement in the United States and United Kingdom." *Mind, Culture, and Activity*, 20, 4: 35 8–371.

Mocombe, Paul C. and Carol Tomlin (2013). *Language, Literacy, and Pedagogy in Postindustrial Societies: The Case of Black Academic Underachievement*. Routledge Research in Education (Vol. 97). New York and London: Routledge.

Mocombe, Paul C. (2012). *Liberal Bourgeois Protestantism: The Metaphysics of Globalization*. Studies in Critical Social Sciences (Vol. 41). Leiden, Netherlands: Brill Publications.

Mocombe, Paul C. and Carol Tomlin (2010). *Oppositional Culture Theory*. Maryland: University Press of America.

Mocombe, Paul C. (2009). *The Liberal Black Protestant Heterosexual Bourgeois Male: From W.E.B. Du Bois to Barack Obama*. Maryland: University Press of America. Mocombe, Paul C. (2008). *The Soulless Souls of Black Folk: A Sociological Reconsideration of Black Consciousness as Du Boisian Double Consciousness*. Maryland: University Press of America.

Model, S. and Fisher, G. (2002) Unions between Blacks and Whites: England and the US Compared. *Ethnic and Racial Studies* 25 (5) pp 72 8–754.

Modood, T., Berthoud, R., Lakey, J., Nazroo, J., Smith, P., Virdee, S. and Beishon, S. (1997) *Ethnic Minorities in Britain: Diversity and Disadvantage*. Policy Studies Institute, London.

Moore, Jerry D. (1997). *Visions of Culture: An Introduction to Anthropological Theories and Theorists*. Walnut Creek, California: AltaMira Press.

Moynihan, Daniel P. (1965). The Negro Family. Washington, D.C.: Office of Planning and Research, US Department of Labor.

Mullard, C. (1982) 'Multiracial Education in Britain: from Assimilation to Cultural Pluralism' in J. (Ed.) (1982) Race, Migration and Schooling.pp.12 0–33. London: Holt, Rinehart and Winston.

Murray, Charles (1984). *Losing Ground: American Social Policy 195 0–1980*. New York: Basic Books.

Murray, R.N. & Gbedemah, G.L (1983) *Foundations of Education in the Caribbean*. London: Hodder & Stoughton.

Myrdal, Gunnar (1944). *An American Dilemma: The Negro Problem and Modern Democracy*. New York: Harper & Row Publishers.

Nash, Gary B. (1972). "Red, White and Black: The Origins of Racism in Colonial America." In Donald Noel (Ed.), *The Origins of American Slavery and Racism* (pp. 13 1–152). Ohio: Charles E. Merrill Publishing Co.

Nicholls, David (1979). *From Dessalines to Duvalier: Race, Colour, and National Independence in Haiti*. New Jersey: Rutgers University Press.

Nietzsche, Friedrich (1956). *The Birth of Tragedy* and *The Genealogy of Morals* (Francis Golffing, Trans.). New York: Anchor Books.

Nobles, Wade (1987). *African American Families: Issues, Ideas, and Insights*. Oakland: Black Family Institute.

Noel, Donald L. (Ed.) (1972). *The Origins of American Slavery and Racism*. Columbus, Ohio: Charles E. Merrill Publishing Co.

Noel, Donald L. (1972). "A Theory of the Origins of Ethnic Stratification." In Donald Noel (Ed.), *The Origins of American Slavery and Racism* (pp. 10 6–127). Ohio: Charles E. Merrill Publishing Co.

Noel, Donald L. (1972). "Slavery and the Rise of Racism." In Donald Noel (Ed.), *The Origins of American Slavery and Racism* (pp. 15 3–174). Ohio: Charles E. Merrill Publishing Co.

Obeyesekere, Gananath (1997 [1992]). *The Apotheosis of Captain Cook: European Mythmaking in the Pacific*. Hawaii: Bishop Museum Press.

Ortner, Sherry (1984). "Theory in Anthropology Since the Sixties," *Comparative Studies in Society and History* 26: 12 6–66.

Outlaw, Lucius (1996). "Conserve" Races?: In Defense of W.E.B. Du Bois." In Bernard W. Bell et al (Eds.), *W.E.B. Du Bois on Race and Culture: Philosophy, Politics, and Poetics* (pp. 1 5–38). New York and London: Routledge.

Parsons, Talcott (1951). *The Social System*. Glencoe, Illinois: Free Press.

Parsons, Talcott (1954). *Essays in Sociological Theory*. Glencoe, Illinois: Free Press.
Parsons, Talcott (1977). *Social Systems and the Evolutions of Action Theory*. New York: Free Press.
Patterson, Orlando (1982). *Slavery and Social Death: A Comparative Study*. Cambridge, Massachusetts: Harvard University Press.
Peach, C. (1968) *West Indian Migration to Britain*: A Social Geography. London: Oxford University Press.
Peach, C. (Ed.) (1996a) *The Ethnic Minority Populations of Great Britain*: Volume 2 of the Ethnicity in the 1991 Census. Office for National Statistics. London: HMSO.
Phillips, U.B. (1918). *American Negro Slavery: A survey of the Supply, Employment, and Control of Negro Labor as Determined by the Plantation Regime*. New York: D. Appleton and Company.
Phillips, U.B. (1963). *Life and Labor in the Old South*. Boston: Little Brown.
Pierre-Louis, Francois (2000). "Decentralization and Democracy in Haiti," paper presented at the International Conference on Democratic Decentralization May 23rd-29th, 2000 Kerala, India.
Polanyi, Karl (2001 [1944]). *The Great Transformation: The Political and Economic Origins of Our Time*. Boston: Beacon Press.
Pollard, V. (1994). *Dread Talk: The Language of Rastafari*. Barbados, Jamaica, Trindad and Tobago: Canoe Press.
Power, S., Edwards, T., Whitty, G. & Wigfall, V. (2003) *Education and the Middle Class* Buckingham, Milton Keynes: Open University Press.
Price-Mars, Jean (1928). Ainsi Parla L' Oncle. Port-au-Prince: Imprimeria de Compiégne.
Psathas, George (1989). *Phenomenology and Sociology: Theory and Research*. Washington, D.C.: University Press of America.
Ramsey, Kate (2014). *The Spirits and the Law: Vodou and Power in Haiti*. Chicago: University of Chicago Press.
Rao, Hayagreeva et al (2005). "Border Crossing: Bricolage and the Erosion of Categorical Boundaries in French Gastronomy," *American Sociological Review* 70: 96 8–991.
Reed, Adolph L. (1997). *W.E.B. Du Bois and American Political Thought: Fabianism and the Color Line*. New York and Oxford: Oxford University Press.
Reyna, Stephen P. (1997). "Theory in Anthropology in the Nineties," *Cultural Dynamics* 9 (3): 32 5–350.
Rex, J. & Moore, R. (1967) *Race, Community & Conflict*. London: Oxford University Press.
Rigaud, Milo (1985). *Secrets of Voodoo*. San Francisco, CA: City Lights Books.
Roediger, David R. (1999). *The Wages of Whiteness: Race and the Making of the American Working Class*. London and New York: Verso.
Rose, Sonya O. (1997). "Class Formation and the Quintessential Worker." In John R. Hall (Ed.), *Reworking Class* (pp. 13 3–166). Ithaca and London: Cornell University Press.
Rosen, H., and Burgess T. (1980). *Language and Dialects of London School Children*. London: Ward, Lock Educational.
Rosenau, Pauline Marie (1992). *Post-Modernism and the Social Sciences: Insights, Inroads, and Intrusions*. Princeton, New Jersey: Princeton University Press.
Roumain, Jacques S. (1940). "The Southeast and the West Indies." *In Prehistoric Patterns in the New World*, edited by Gordon R. Wiley, 16 5–72. New York: Viking Fund Publications in Anthropology.
Rubin, Vera (Ed.) (1960). *Caribbean Studies: A Symposium*. Seattle: University of Washington Press.
Sahlins, Marshall (1995a). *How "Natives" Think: About Captain Cook, For Example*. Chicago: University of Chicago Press.
Sahlins, Marshall (1995b). *Historical Metaphors and Mythical Realities*. Ann Arbor: University of Michigan Press.
Sahlins, Marshall (1990). "The Political Economy of Grandeur in Hawaii from 181 0–1830." In Emiko Ohnuki-Tierney (Ed.), *Culture through Time: Anthropological Approaches* (pp. 2 6–56). California: Stanford University Press.

Sahlins, Marshall (1989). "Captain Cook at Hawaii," *The Journal of the Polynesian Society* 98; 4: 37 1–423.
Sahlins, Marshall (1985). *Islands of History*. Chicago: University of Chicago Press.
Sahlins, Marshall (1982). "The Apotheosis of Captain Cook." In Michel Izard and Pierre Smith (Eds.), *Between Belief and Transgression* (pp. 7 3–102). Chicago: University of Chicago Press.
Sahlins, Marshall (1976). *Culture and Practical Reason*. Chicago, IL: University of Chicago Press.
Said, Edward (1979). *Orientalism*. New York: Vintage Books.
Sarup, Madan (1993). *An Introductory Guide to Post-Structuralism and Postmodernism* (second edition). Athens: The University of Georgia Press.
Saussure de, Ferdinand (1972 [1916]. *Course in General Linguistics*, Edited by Charles Bally et al. Illinois: Open Court.
Sertima, Ivan V. ([1979] 1989). *They Came Before Columbus*. New York: Random House.
Schutz, Alfred (1978). "Phenomenology and the Social Sciences." In Thomas Luckmann (Ed.), *Phenomenology and Sociology: Selected Readings* (pp. 11 9–141). New York: Penguin Books.
Schutz, Alfred (1978). "Some Structures of the Life-World." In Thomas Luckmann (Ed.), *Phenomenology and Sociology: Selected Readings* (pp. 25 7–274). New York: Penguin Books.
Schwalbe, Michael L. (1993). "Goffman Against Postmodernism: Emotion and the Reality of the Self." *Symbolic Interaction* 16(4): 33 3–350.
Searle, John R. (1997). *The Mystery of Consciousness*. New York: The New York Review of Books.
Sebba, M. (1993). *London Jamaican*. London: Longman.
Sebba, M. (2007) *Caribbean Creoles and Black English*. In D. Britain (Ed.) *Languages in the British Isles: Language in the British Isles*. (pp. 27 6–292). Cambridge: Cambridge University Press.
Sennett, Richard (1998). *The Corrosion of Character*. New York: W.W. Norton & Company.
Slemon, Stephen (1995). "The Scramble for Post-colonialism." In Bill Ashcroft et al (Eds.), The Post-colonial Studies Reader (pp. 4 5–52). London and New York: Routledge.
Smedley, Audrey (1999). *Race in North America: Origin and Evolution of a Worldview* (Second edition). Boulder, Colorado: Westview Press.
Smiley Group, Inc. (2006). *The Covenant with Black America*. Chicago: Third World Press.
Smith M.G. (1960). "The African Heritage in the Caribbean." In Vera Rubin (Ed.), *Caribbean Studies: A Symposium* (pp. 3 4–46). Seattle: University of Washington Press.
Solomon, Robert C. (1988). *A History of Western Philosophy: Continental Philosophy Since 1750, The Rise and Fall of the Self*. Oxford: Oxford University Press.
Sowell, Thomas (1975). *Race and Economics*. New York: David McKay.
Sowell, Thomas (1981). *Ethnic America*. New York: Basic Books.
Spivak, Chakravorty Gayatri (1994 [1988]). "Can the Subaltern Speak?" In Patrick Williams and Laura Chrisma (Eds.), *Colonial Discourse and Post-Colonial Theory A Reader* (pp. 6 6–111). New York: Columbia University Press.
Stack, Carol B. (1974). *All Our Kin: Strategies for Survival in a Black Community*. New York: Harper & Row Publishers.
Stampp, Kenneth (1967). *The Peculiar Institution*. New York: Alfred Knopf, Inc.
Strand, S. (2012) The White British-Black Caribbean Achievement Gap: Tests, Tiers and Teacher Expectations. *British Educational Research Journal* 28 (1): pp. 7 5–101.
Staples, Robert (ed.) (1978). *The Black Family: Essays and Studies*. California: Wadsworth Publishing Company.
Stewart, David and Algis Mickunas (1990). *Exploring Phenomenology: A Guide to the Field and its Literature* (Second edition). Athens: Ohio University Press.
Strauss, Claudia and Naomi Quinn (1997). *A Cognitive Theory of Cultural Meaning*. United Kingdom: Cambridge University Press.
Stone, M. (1981) *Education and the Black Child: the Myth of Multicultural Education*. London: Fontana.

Stuckey, Sterling (1987). *Slave Culture: Nationalist Theory and the Foundations of Black America*. New York and Oxford: Oxford University Press.

Sturrock, John (ed.) (1979). *Structuralism and Since: From Lévi-Strauss to Derrida*. Oxford: Oxford University Press.

Sudarkasa, Niara (1980). "African and Afro-American Family Structure: A Comparison," The *Black Scholar*, 11: 3 7–60.

Sudarkasa, Niara (1981). "Interpreting the African Heritage in Afro-American Family Organization." In Harriette P. McAdoo (Ed.), *Black Families*. California: Sage Publications.

Sundquist, Eric J. (ed.) (1996). *The Oxford W.E.B. Du Bois Reader*. New York and Oxford: Oxford University Press.

Sutcliffe, D. (1992). *Systems in Black Language*. Avon, Clevedon: Multilingual Matters.

Swann Report (1985) *Education for all: Report of the Committee of Inquiry into the Education of children from Minority Ethnic Groups*. London: HMSO.

Thomas, Nicholas (1982). "A Cultural Appropriation of History? Sahlins Among the Hawaiians," *Canberra Anthropology* 5; 1: 6 0–65.

Thompson, E.P. (1964). *The Making of the English Working Class*. New York: Pantheon Books.

Thompson, E.P. (1978). *The Poverty of Theory and Other Essays*. New York: Monthly Review Press.

Tomlin, C. (1988). "Black Preaching Style". MPhil thesis. University of Birmingham, Birmingham.

Tomlin, C. (1999). *Black Language Style in Sacred and Secular Contexts*. Medgar Evers College (CUNY): Caribbean Diaspora Press.

Tomlinson, S. (1984) *Home and School in Multicultural Britain*. London: Batsford.

Tomlinson, S. (2001) Education in a Post-welfare Society. Buckingham: Open University Press.

Tomlinson, S. (2008) *Race & Education: Policy & Politics in Britain*. Maidenhead, Berkshire: Open University Press.

Tomlinson, S. (2011) More Radical Reform (but don't mention race) Gaps and Silences in the Government's Discourse. *Race Equality Teaching* 29 (2): 2 5–29.

Townsend, H.E.R. (1971) Immigrants in England: The LEA Response: Slough: National Foundation for Educational Research.

Trouillot, Michel-Rolph (1995). *Silencing the Past: Power and the Production of History*. Boston, Massachusetts: Beacon Press.

Troyna, B. (1979) Differential Commitment to Ethnic Identity by Black Youths in Britain. *New Community* (7): 40 6–414.

Troyna, B. (1993) *Racism and Education: Research Perspectives*. Buckingham: Open University Press.

Troyna, B. Smith, D.I. (Eds.) (1983) *Racism, School and the Labor Market*. Leicester: National Youth Bureau.

Troyna, B. and Carrington, B. (1990) *Education, Racism and Reform*: London: Routledge.

Trudgill, P. (1990). *Sociolinguistics: An Introduction*. Harmondsworth: Penguin.

Tulloch, Hugh (1999). *The Debate on the American Civil War Era*. Manchester: Manchester University Press.

Turner, Ralph H. (1976). "The Real Self: From Institution to Impulse." *American Journal of Sociology* 81: 98 9–1016.

Turner, Ralph H. (1988). "Personality in Society: Social Psychology's Contribution to Sociology." *Social Psychology Quarterly* 51; 1: 1–10.

Tussman, Joseph and Jacobus TenBroek (1949). "The Equal Protection of the Laws." *California Law Review* 37;3:34 1–381.

Wallerstein, Immanuel (1982). "The Rise and Future Demise of the World Capitalist System: Concepts for Comparative Analysis." In Hamza Alavi and Teodor Shanin (Eds.), *Introduction to the Sociology of "Developing Societies"* (pp. 2 9–53). New York: Monthly Review Press.

Walvin, J. (1984) Passage to Britain. Harmondsworth: Penguin.

Walvin, J. (1982) Black Ivory: A History of British Slavery. London: Harper Collins.

Ward, Glenn (1997). *Postmodernism*. London: Hodder & Stoughton Ltd.
Warren, S. and Gillborn, D. (2003). *Race Equality and Education in Birmingham*. London: Education Policy Research Unit, Institute of Education.
Watkins, S. Craig (1998). *Representing: Hip-Hop Culture and the Production of Black Cinema*. Chicago: The University of Chicago Press.
Weber, Max (1958 [190 4–1905]). *The Protestant Ethic and the Spirit of Capitalism* (Talcott Parsons, Trans.). New York: Charles Scribner's Sons.
Weinreich, U. (1968). *Language in Contact*. The Hague: Mouton.
West, Cornel (1993). *Race Matters*. New York: Vintage Books.
West, David (1996). *An Introduction to Continental Philosophy*. Cambridge: Polity Press.
Williams, Raymond (1977). *Marxism and Literature*. Oxford: Oxford University Press.
Wilson, Kirt H. (1999). "Towards a Discursive Theory of Racial Identity: The Souls of Black Folk as a Response to Nineteenth-Century Biological Determinism." *Western Journal of Communication*, 63 (2): 19 3–215.
Wilson, William J. (1978). *The Declining Significance of Race: Blacks and Changing American Institutions*. Chicago and London: The University of Chicago Press.
Wilson, William J. (1987). *The Truly Disadvantaged*. Chicago and London: University of Chicago Press.
Winant, Howard (2001). *The World is a Ghetto: Race and Democracy since World War II*. New York: Basic Books.
Winford, D. (1993). *Predication in Caribbean Creoles*. Amsterdam: John Benjamins.
Wittgenstein, Ludwig (2001 [1953]). *Philosophical Investigations* (G.E.M. Anscombe Trans.). Malden, Massachusetts: Blackwell Publishers Ltd.
Wright, Kai (Ed.) (2001). *The African-American Archive: The History of the Black Experience in Documents*. New York: Black Dog & Leventhal Publishers.
Woodson, Carter G. (1969 [1933]). *The Mis-Education of the Negro*. Washington: Associated Publishers Inc.
Youdell, D. (2003) Identity Traps or How Black Students Fail: The Interaction Between Biographical, Sub-cultural and Learner Identities. *British Journal of Sociology of Education* 24 (1): 3–20.
Young, Iris Marion (1994). "Gender as Seriality: Thinking about Women as a Social Collective," *Signs* 19: 71 3–738.
Zamir, Shamoon (1995). *Dark Voices: W.E.B. Du Bois and American Thought, 188 8–1903*. Chicago & London: The University of Chicago Press.
Zeitlin, Irving M. (1990). *Ideology and the development of sociological theory* (4th ed.). Englewood Cliffs, New Jersey: Prentice-Hall.

Index

acculturation: process of, 8, 73, 82; slavery and, 85–86, 87
acting white: hypothesis, 92; Ogbu on, 13–14, 15, 89, 93, 118
adaptive-vitality school, 22–23, 29, 33, 53, 76, 96n12
Africa: African-Americanization of, 117–119; post-emancipation period, 99–107; within Protestant ethic and spirit of capitalism, 99–119; racial-caste-in-class and, 99, 107; social class language games and, 99, 100, 102, 103–104, 107, 110, 116–117
African-Americanization: of Africa, Caribbean, and black diaspora, 117–119; causes of, 10, 117; definition of, 2; homogenization or convergence as, 4; hypothesis, 22; impacts of, 19; underclass and, 117–119
African memory retentions, 22
African spirituality, 96n13
Akon, 106
Aldridge, Ira, 108
ambivalence, 21, 25, 28–29, 52, 76
American Dream, 15–17, 118
American hegemony, capitalism under, 1–3, 5, 6–7, 10, 18, 27, 54, 73–75
anti-anti-essentialist school, 22–23, 53, 76
anti-essentialist school, 22–23, 53, 76
Archer, Kevin, 5, 66, 72, 113
Armstrong, Karen, 58

Ashimolowo, Matthew, 106
athletes, 15, 90, 93

Barber, Francis, 107
being: actions deriving from gaze of, 43; being black, 15–17, 93–95, 119; being white, 114
being-in-the-world: forms of, 33, 44, 46, 49, 62, 81, 82; phenomenology of, 38–41
Bergson, Henri, 37
Berthoud, R., 112
BET. *See* Black Entertainment Television
Bhabha, Homi, 73
Blackaby, D.H., 112
Black/African American English Vernacular, 14, 81, 90, 92, 93
black America: within Protestant ethic and spirit of capitalism, 77–95; today, 88–95
black bourgeoisie: blacks in UK, 107; definition of, 1–2; education and, 116–117; post-emancipation period and, 100, 102, 103–105; post-war migration and, 110; underclass compared to, 2–3, 11, 14, 18, 21, 24, 26–27, 29, 52–54, 91, 92–95
Black British Talk, 110, 114
black consciousnesses and identities, 21–29, 81

black diaspora, African-Americanization of, 117–119
Black Entertainment Television (BET), 15–17, 93–95, 119
black nationalism, 86, 87, 108–109
blackness: definition of, 1–2, 92, 113–114; Du Bois on, 1; economic status of, 93–95, 119
blacks: being black, 15–17, 93–95, 119; in UK, 22–23, 107–109
black social agency, 22, 31–32
Blassingame, John, 85
"Bling bling", 15, 15–17, 118–119
Bourdieu, Pierre: on capital, 13, 89, 96n16; on phenomenological structuralism, 32–33
Boyson, R., 116
Bryant, Jamal, 106
Burrell, Kim, 106
Bynum, Juanita, 2–3, 10, 11, 15, 17, 106, 118, 119

capital: accumulation of, 10, 12, 25, 27, 28–29, 32, 52–54, 59, 62, 63–64, 71, 75–76; Bourdieu on, 13, 89, 96n16
capitalism: under American hegemony, 1–3, 5, 6–7, 10, 18, 27, 54, 73–75; Mocombe on, 6; post-industrial, 13, 15–17, 28, 59, 89, 92, 93–95, 119; theories on, 6–7. *See also* Protestant ethic and spirit of capitalism
Caribbean: African-Americanization of, 117–119; post-emancipation period, 99–107; within Protestant ethic and spirit of capitalism, 99–119; racial-caste-in-class and, 99, 107; social class language games and, 99, 100, 102, 103–104, 107, 110, 116–117
Cartesian transcendental intellectual activity, 23–25
Cheung, S., 112
Christianity, 57–59, 68; evangelism, 17, 58, 59, 84, 95n8, 106, 117, 119
church and state, marriage of, 62
cities, work in, 11, 90–91
Civil Rights Act (1964), 27–28, 75
civil rights legislation, 9–10, 27, 75
civil rights movement, 9, 26–27, 75
Civil War, 24, 82, 87–88, 90, 93–95

class racism, 83
Collins, Patricia Hill: on black consciousnesses and identities, 23, 24–25, 25–27; on globalization, 73–75
colonialism: globalization and, 67–70; Said on, 54n2; Slemon on, 45, 54n2
comprador bourgeoisie, 1, 8
consciousness: black consciousnesses and identities, 21–29, 81; phenomenological structuralism and, 31–54; social class language games and, 3, 4; transcendental ego of, 33, 36–37, 39, 41, 42–43, 50. *See also* double consciousness
consumerism: globalization and, 12; middle class and, 71
convergence: homogenization and, 4, 8, 73; theory, 7–9
Cox, C.B., 116
créolité, 21, 25, 28–29, 52
critical race theory, 23
Cromwell, Oliver, 61
culture: of globalization, 5–6, 6–7, 66–67, 73; globalization as, 6, 6–8, 66, 72, 73. *See also* hip-hop culture
Curray, William, 108

dark matter, 34
Dasein, Heidegger on, 37, 39–41
decentered subject, 25–26, 31, 73–75
Delaney, Martin Robinson, 1, 86
deportation, 2, 10
Derrida, Jacques, 25–26, 33
De Saussure, Ferdinand, 54n2, 55n5
Dessalines, Jean-Jacques, 1
development model, 4–5, 67, 69, 70–71
différance, 33
discrimination: blacks in UK, 108–109; against others, 28, 61; outlawing and banning of, 27, 75, 111, 112
Dodgson, Elyse, 109
Dollar, Creflo, 3, 10, 11, 15, 17, 106, 118, 119
Domhoff, William, 4
double consciousness: Du Bois on, 23–24, 26, 52, 87, 93–95; Gilroy on, 52, 93–95; theory of, 21, 25, 28–29, 52; West on, 52, 93–95
Douglas, Frederick, 1

Drummond, Andre, 106
Du Bois, W.E.B.: on blackness, 1; on double consciousness, 23–24, 26, 52, 87, 93–95; leadership of, 27, 75
Dutty, Boukman, 1
Dyson, Michael Eric, 2–3, 15

East African Hip Hop (Ntarangwi), 119
education: black bourgeoisie and, 116–117; during post-emancipation period, 104–105; racial-caste-in-class and, 116; theory, 93–95, 96n16; in UK, 115–117; underachievement in, 13–14, 89–93, 116, 117; underclass and, 116–117
élan vital, 37, 41, 42
Elie, Mario, 106
Elkins, Stanley, 85, 86
English: Black/African American English Vernacular, 14, 81, 90, 92, 93; Standard, 14, 81, 90; Standard British, 110
Enlightenment, 64–65
entertainment industry, 15, 90–93, 107, 118, 119
EPR paradox, 34
Equiano, Olaudah, 107
evangelism, 17, 58, 59, 84, 95n8, 106, 117, 119
Ewing, Patrick, 106
Eysenck, Hans, 116

Fanon, Frantz, 1, 8, 23
force, globalization as ideological and material, 5
Foucault, Michel, 25–26
Frankfort School, 23
Frazier, E. Franklin, 1, 96n13–96n14
freedoms, human rights and, 26, 27–28
Freud, Sigmund, 36

Garnett, Henry Highland, 1, 86
Garvey, Marcus, 1
Geist, Hegel on, 34–36
general relativity, theory of, 36
Giddens, Anthony, 32
Gilroy, Paul: on black consciousnesses and identities, 23–24, 26–27; on double consciousness, 52, 93–95; on globalization, 73–75
globalization, 66–76; age of, 2, 3, 4, 7, 21, 54, 105; Collins on, 73–75; colonialism and, 67–70; consumerism and, 12; as culture, 6, 6–8, 66, 72, 73; culture of, 5–6, 6–7, 66–67, 73; development model and, 4–5, 67, 69, 70–71; Gilroy on, 73–75; homogenization and, 67, 68, 73, 73–75; hooks on, 73–75; as ideological force and material force, 5; impacts of, 2, 3, 8–10; processes of, 7, 27–28; theories, 12; West on, 73–75
God, understanding of, 57–58, 58
god particle (Higgs Boson Field), 34–36, 44

Habermas, Jürgen: on capital accumulation, 62, 63; praxis school and, 32
Haitian Revolution, 47
Hall, Stuart, 73
Harding, Vincent D., 84
Harvey, David, 67, 72
Heath, A., 112
Hegel, G.W.F., 34–36
Heidegger, Martin: on *Dasein*, 37, 39–41; phenomenology of, 38–42; on ready-to-hand, unready-to-hand, present-at-hand stances, 37, 39–41
Higgs Boson Field (god particle), 34–36, 44
hip-hop culture: influences, 15–17, 93, 114, 117; underclass and, 14–15, 18, 91–92
homogenization: convergence and, 4, 8, 73; globalization and, 67, 68, 73, 73–75
hooks, bell: on black consciousnesses and identities, 23, 24, 25–27; on globalization, 73–75
housing, in UK, 114–115
human rights, freedoms and, 26, 27–28
Husserl, Edmund, 36, 39
hybridity, 21, 25, 29, 52, 76
hybridization: impacts of, 8, 8–9, 73–75; social integration and, 27, 75

identity: black consciousnesses and, 21–29, 81; identity-in-differential, 22;

identity politics, 27, 29, 73–75, 104, 117; of middle class, 113–114
IMF. *See* International Monetary Fund
immigration: deportation and, 2, 10; patterns, 99, 105, 107; post-war migration to UK, 109–110; restrictions, 109–110
Industrial Revolution, 108
instant gratification, 15
institutional regulators, 45–46, 48–50, 55n5, 77, 80, 83
integration: of children, into social class language games, 12; of others, 12, 27. *See also* social integration
International Monetary Fund (IMF), 4, 11, 62
intersectionality, 21, 25, 26, 28–29, 52, 76, 93–95
Islamic fundamentalists, 47

Jakes, TD, 3, 10, 11, 15, 17, 106, 118, 119
Jameson, Fredric, 67, 72
Jean, Wyclef, 106, 119
Jensen, Arthur, 116
Jesus, gospel of, 58–59
Jones, Noel, 106
Joshua, Temitope B., 106

Karenga, Maulana, 78
King, Martin Luther, Jr., 27, 75

labor: market, in UK, 111–114; outsourcing and exploitation of, 12–13
Lacan, Jacques, 36, 43
language game, 39, 42. *See also* social class language games
League of Colored People, 108
Long, Eddie, 3, 10, 11, 15, 106, 118, 119
Lumumba, Patrice, 1

Macann, Christopher, 42
Marx, Karl: on materialism, 39, 44; praxis school and, 32; theory of, 60; on world-systems theory, 5
master/slave relationship, 45, 47, 80, 85, 87, 95n3, 95n9
materialism, 39, 44
McClurkin, Donnie, 106
McIntosh, Neil, 111

McMichael, Philip, 68, 69–70
meaning: deferment of, 8, 19, 25, 29, 33, 37, 38, 42, 43, 45, 53, 64, 73–75, 76, 80, 100, 104, 110; indeterminacy of, 25–26, 31–32, 36, 52
media, 3, 10, 15–17, 118, 119
Merleau-Ponty, Maurice, 37, 39
middle class: consumerism and, 71; identity of, 113–114; upper class and, 7–8, 13, 89, 113
Mocombe, Paul C.: on capitalism, 6; on phenomenological structuralism, 21–22, 32, 33, 34–37, 39–41, 53, 54n1–54n2; work of, 7, 15–17
modernity, 57–76
Moody, Harold, 108
multiverses (parallel universes), 34–37, 41–42
Munroe, Myles, 106
Mutumbo, Dikembe, 106

nation state: building era, 100; retrenchment of, 1, 6, 8, 8–9, 10
nature, four forces of, 34
négritude, 21, 25, 28–29, 52
Negro church, 96n13
Negro Convention Movement, 96n11
Neli, 111, 113
neoliberalism: emphasis of, 65; impacts of, 5; racial-caste-in-class and, 12–13
Ntarangwi, Mwenda, 119

Obama, Barack, 27, 75
Ogbu, John, 13–14, 15, 89, 93, 118
others: discrimination against, 28, 61; multiethnic, multicultural, multiracial, embourgeoised, 8; participation or integration of, 12, 27; socialization of, 9
outsourcing: impacts of, 6, 8, 10, 13, 27, 75, 90–91; labor exploitation and, 12–13
Oyakhilome, Christian, 106
Oyedepo, David, 106

Pan-African movement, 108
parallel universes (multiverses), 34–37, 41–42
pathological-pathogenic school, 22–23, 29, 33, 53, 76, 96n12

Pétion, Alexander, 1
phenomenological structuralism:
    background on, 32–34; Bourdieu on,
    32–33; consciousness and, 31–54;
    diagrammatically, 44–48, 49, 51, 54n4;
    discussion and conclusions on, 50–54;
    Mocombe on, 21–22, 32, 33, 34–37,
    39–41, 53, 54n1–54n2; power and,
    48–50, 55n7; rules of conduct and,
    45–46, 46–47, 48; social class language
    games and, 36, 39, 42–44, 47, 48, 52;
    space-time and, 34–36, 41; subatomic
    particles and, 34–38, 41–44, 45, 50–52;
    theory of, 34–44
Philosophical Investigations
    (Wittgenstein), 42
Pierre-Paul, Jason, 106
post-emancipation period, 99–107
post-war migration, to UK, 109–110
power: elites, 3, 10, 15, 45–46, 48, 50, 65,
    69, 79–80, 118; phenomenological
    structuralism and, 48–50, 55n7
praxis school, 32
predestination, 61, 63–64, 79–80, 87
present-at-hand stance, 37, 38, 39–41, 44,
    45, 53
prosperity gospel: promotion of, 17, 88,
    119; theory of, 3, 11, 15–17
Prosser, Gabriel, 84, 86
Protestant ethic and spirit of capitalism:
    African and Caribbean life within,
    99–119; black America within, 77–95;
    impacts of, 2, 3, 10, 15; modernity via,
    57–76; theories on, 4, 7, 8–9, 18; Weber
    on, 7, 44, 59, 60–61, 63, 73, 88
Protestant Reformation, 58, 61
*The Protestant Ethic and the Spirit of
    Capitalism* (Weber), 7

quantum mechanics, 34–36, 42

racial-caste-in-class: Africa, Caribbean
    and, 99, 107; creation of, 24, 52–53, 86,
    99; education and, 116; neoliberalism
    and, 12–13; post-war migration and,
    110
racial-class lines differentiation, 1–2, 10,
    17, 79
radicalism, 65–66

rap music, 17, 106
ready-to-hand stance, 37, 38, 39–41, 44,
    45, 53
Rihanna, 106, 119
role models, 17–18, 118
Rollock, Nicola, 113
Roosevelt New Deal Era, 10
Rostow, W.W., 70
rules of conduct: formulation of, 62;
    phenomenological structuralism and,
    45–46, 46–47, 48; slavery and, 85,
    86–87, 96n10

Sahlins, Marshall, 32
Said, Edward, 54n2, 73
Sankara, Thomas, 1
Sartre, Jean-Paul, 37, 41
Seacole, Mary, 108
service economies, 29, 53, 76
service occupations, 9, 12, 13, 27, 67,
    71–72, 92
Simpson, Ludi, 112
Sklair, Leslie, 13
slavery: acculturation and, 85–86, 87;
    laws, 83–84, 95n7; master/slave
    relationship during, 45, 47, 80, 85, 87,
    95n3, 95n9; post-emancipation period
    and, 99–107; racial-class lines
    differentiation and, 1–2, 10, 17; revolts
    and resistance to, 84; rules of conduct
    and, 85, 86–87, 96n10; "seasoning"
    process, 85, 87; slave and free Negro
    population, 83; slave trade, 77, 81, 82,
    95n9, 107, 108; theories on, 77–88,
    95n3–95n4, 96n12, 96n14
The Slave Community (Blassingame), 85
Slemon, Stephen, 45, 54n2
Smalls, Biggie, 106, 119
Smith, David, 111
social class language games: Africa,
    Caribbean and, 99, 100, 102, 103–104,
    107, 110, 116–117; children integrated
    into, 12; differentiation into, 13, 18, 21,
    24, 29, 82, 90–91; ideology, practical
    consciousness, and language of, 3, 4;
    phenomenological structuralism and,
    36, 39, 42–44, 47, 48, 52;
    reinforcement and reproduction of, 11;
    transportation into, 80–81

social integration: forms of, 2; hybridization and, 27, 75; logic of, 7, 8
social reproduction theory, 96n16
space-time: coordinates, 6, 72; phenomenological structuralism and, 34–36, 41
Spivak, Gayatri, 22
Standard British English, 110
Standard English, 14, 81, 90
subatomic particles, 34–38, 41–44, 45, 50–52
supersymmetry theory, 34

televangelisms, 106, 117, 118
Tomlinson, John, 73
Trade Union Movement, 108
transcendental ego, of consciousness, 33, 36–37, 39, 41, 42–43, 50
transnational capitalist class, 13
Troyna, B., 111
Turner, Nat, 84, 86

UK. *See* United Kingdom
underclass: African-Americanization and, 117–119; black bourgeoisie compared to, 2–3, 11, 14, 18, 21, 24, 26–27, 29, 52–54, 91, 92–95; blacks in UK, 107; characteristics of, 13, 17, 89, 90–95, 114; education and, 116–117; hip-hop culture and, 14–15, 18, 91–92; post-emancipation period and, 100, 102–105; post-war migration and, 110
United Kingdom (UK): blacks in, 22–23, 107–109; education in, 115–117; housing in, 114–115; ideologies, policies and practices in, 110–111; labor market in, 111–114; post-war migration to, 109–110
United Nations, 5, 9, 62
universal ontological structure, 41
unready-to-hand stance, 37, 38, 39–41, 44, 45, 53
upper class: commodification by, 6, 67, 92; domination by, 117; middle class and, 7–8, 13, 89, 113
upward mobility, 15–17, 90–93, 118

Vesey, Denmark, 84, 86

Walker, David, 86
Wallerstein, Immanuel, 5, 71
Walvin, J., 108
Washington, Booker T., 1, 86
Water, Billy, 107
WB. *See* World Bank
Weber, Max: on Protestant ethic and spirit of capitalism, 7, 44, 59, 60–61, 63, 73, 88; *The Protestant Ethic and the Spirit of Capitalism*, 7
Wells, Ida B., 1
West, Cornel: on black consciousnesses and identities, 23–24, 26–27; on double consciousness, 52, 93–95; on globalization, 73–75
white: acting white, 13–14, 15, 89, 92, 93, 118; being white, 114
Who Rules America (Domhoff), 4
Wittgenstein, Ludwig: on language game, 39, 42; *Philosophical Investigations*, 42
Woodson, Carter G., 1
World Bank (WB), 4, 11, 62, 71
World Development Report 1980 (WB), 71
world-systems theory, 5, 67, 71
World Trade Organization (WTO), 4